C000138656

Forward

Just after deciding to settle down to write this book I was informed that someone from Canklow had just released a book about the same area, covering the same era. This sort of stopped me in my tracks. Curious to compare notes I went out and purchased the book called "Canklow Born and Bred" by Author John Winwood, and what a good read it was, and would certainly recommend it as a book to read.

John was born the same year as me at the opposite end of the estate, so really Johns stories and mine should be more or less identical. Well in a way they are, but seen through a different set of eyes. You see john was everything I wasn't, sportsman, athlete, a good all-rounder, whereas I was useless couldn't kick or catch a ball and could run fast only if a Park Keeper was chasing me. The more I read of his book convinced me I needed to write mine.

The best comparison I could come up with was, John was like Roy of the Rovers and me like Denis the Menace.

Preface

I would not have been able to write this book, had it not been for the quick reactions of my wife and daughter. Combined with the excellent staff at the Sheffield Royal Hallamshire Hospital.

Early in the new millennium i had the misfortune to suffer a brain hemorrhage. No prior warning, totally out of the blue. Not wanting to go into detail, the outcome of this incident resulted in the loss of my long and short term memory. Which is much better than the alternative which was Dead. After six months rehabilitation, I was assessed by the Senior Brain Surgeon. His prognosis was that I had made a good recovery, but he stated that the level I had reached would not improve any further, but neither would it deteriorate. This was a cause of concern to me, as my memory had nowhere near fully recovered and was at best, very sketchy.

I could not remember peoples names, even close friends and family. Neither could I remember things from my past. Unless someone reminded me of an incident or occasion, then I would recall it.

The best way I can find describe the situation I found my self in is. If you imagine your memory is a drawer in a filing cabinet. Someone takes out the memory drawer and tips the memory files onto the floor. Then collects them back up and puts the back in the drawer but in no particular order.

Similar to the famous Morcambe and Wise Quote. My memories were all in there, but not necessarily in the right order

It was only when someone reminded me of a memory, that memory got filed in its proper place.

I became depressed at the thought of not getting my memory back, and being a staunch and stubborn Yorshireman, I was determined to prove the surgeon wrong. The first part of the journey to regain my memory, was when my wife bought me a rusty 1965 Lambretta scooter. We used be Mods, during the swinging sixties.

How was this going to help regain my memory?

Well the scooter, I was told, was complete, but in bits. All the parts were delivered in a large crate, the only item missing was the instructions on how to put it all together.

What a challenge, but you can see the results in the book, as the scooter shown is the actual one I built, and is a replica of the one I had in 1964.

I hope this book makes you remember your past with a smile, a laugh, and maybe even a tear. This book is proof that you should never give in to a *prognosis*. My memory is not back to what it was, but that may just be because of aging. But its a dam sight better than it was when I left the Hospital.

If this encounter has taught me anything, and remember, there is not much you can teach a Yorkshireman, its, Live for today. Tomorrow might not arrive, in this life there are no guarantees.

Prognosis is a medical term for predicting the likely or expected development of a disease, including whether the signs and symptoms will improve or worsen or remain stable over time; expectations of quality of life, such as the ability to carry out daily activities; the potential for complications and associated health issues; and the likelihood of survival. ...

Instructions

I know Books don't usually come with instructions but this book does. If yer from Canklow tha dunt need em. If you are from other parts of Rotherham i.e. Broom Valley, Tha might need a refresher. If you are from any other part of Yorkshire. In general as above applies. If you are not from Yorkshire but fancy being a pseudo Yorkshireman, then these instructions are definitely for thee.

Read the stories as they are written. Words are often shortened or letters missed out completely. For instance, using the letter G is often a waste of time, so it gets left out of a word. Swimming becomes Swimmin so most words endin in ing get this treatment.   Read what you see an don't over complicate it, say it as it ses.

Before you get started on this book, here's a couple o sentence's to practice on.

He ses itintis bur I ber it is. Translation :- He says it does not belong to him but I bet it does.   Lerus gerus hansweshed Translation :- Let us wash our hands.

Keep it simple n say wat tha sees, n you'l soon bi speekin Yorkshire like a guddun.
For Additional Yorksherisms see the Glossary

Chapter 1 The Early Years.The Black Sheep, White Boots, and a Sex Scandal.

The Black Sheep

If wi ant ad thee wi wud own a row of houses bi na. This was a comment mi Mum would often make when I came in from playing, the arse end of mi trousers ripped out, an the soles of mi shoes hangin off.

Born in November 1946 some 12 years after my elder Brother Peter, "Mummy's favored one" and 7 years before my younger sister Kathryn "Daddy's little Princess". I suppose I was the genuine Black Sheep of the family. I did not become aware of this mantle until much later in life, and on reflection, I considered myself an ordinary kid, that lived in Canklow.

For those who don't know Rotherham. Canklow is a Council Estate which gained a reputation, during and after the war years, as a somewhat shady area, with lots of even shadier characters, and generally described by other residents of Rotherham, in polite terms, as rough.

I grew up in Canklow in the 40s 50s and 60s and for me it was home. To me, it was, and as far as I knew, no different to any other area in Rotherham.

I was too young to understand class, rank, rich, poor. As far as I was concerned everyone in Rotherham lived the same as me. The first time I realised that some people lived differently, was when, at the age of 15.

Ray Brough, a workmate of mine, invited me to his "detached" house for tea. We had Salmon and Cucumber sandwiches, cut diagonally? A cup of real coffee, not Camp coffee with "added chicory" like ours

Rays mum asked me if I would like watermelon for dessert. Panic strikes, what the bloody hell is a watermelon? Yes please, came my reply, not knowing what to expect. When it arrived I was pleasantly surprised. It wer all reyt, and still love it to this day.
A 15 year old, eating triangular real Salmon sandwiches, drinkin proper coffee, and eytin watermelon, in a detached house. Had I become middle class?

What follows is my take on a childhood through to adulthood, free from the worries and threats of the modern world, without the gadgets, and gizmos, with very little money to spare. Where manners cost nothing. Even in a place like Canklow "please" and "thank you" were obligatory and "respect your elders" was a law you broke at your own peril.

Something lost on the young of the modern world

White Boots and a Sex Scandal.

If you were asked "What is your earliest childhood memory." What would your answer be? For me that first memory was "White Boots. I was about four years old when I was given a brand new pair of White boots. White boots remind me of Whitsuntide. It wer the only time of year when I had all new clothes. A wer only allowed to wear em for one day, an then they wer pur away for special occasions. But in that one day, Whit Sunday. I would earn what I would consider a small fortune.Tradition was, you would visit your relatives, and show them how well you scrubbed up.For this visit you would be given a cash gift, usually Threepence or a Tanner, and occasionally a Bob. I still have no why we were given money, perhaps someone reading this will enlighten me.

This is where being part of a community like Canklow comes to the fore.

Practically every neighbor on your street was classed as Uncle or Auntie, whether they were blood relatives or not, and many others on adjoining streets, and every single one got a visit.

I remember the joy of countin all MY money, just for gerrin dressed up, and staying clean for a day.

I think this was my introduction to my entrepreneurial tendencies. Which will become clear later. Nothing else much comes to mind during my pre-school years except the shocking SEX SCANDAL that left me traumatised for years.

WARNING EXPLICIT CONTENT

A thought long and hard abart this memory, an seein as those so called celebrities allus add a sex scandal into their books to boost sales, a thought ad write abart mi first sexual experience, so that other young kids can be warned.

Bein a Gentleman, and to protect the other person's identity. I will change Angela's name to Kylie, for the purpose of this memory.

A wer abart 4 n half when this append n Kylie wer abart 5 (the older woman).

A wer playin int street by mi sen, when Kylie kem n asked mi if a wanted to play a new game. Allus the one to try sumat new a jumped at the chance. Kylie beckoned me to follow her into t passage at side of her house, as we were walkin in, I asked her what this game wer called.

"Doctors n Nurses" shi sed.

Well ad never erd o that one befoor but a wer willin to ge it a gu. Kylie explained that the game was to remove you clooas from the bottom half of yer body n inspect what wer on show, (Na ya have to remember ere that a were only 4 oh and a half, and had mastered undoin buttons on me short trousers burant mastered fassnin em back up).

Clooas removed the game began. Kylie bent over looked at my bits, nodded her head in appreciation, and smiled. Then it wer my turn. I bent darn, not knowing what to expect, and looked at her bits. That's when a got the shock o me life,.

There wer nowt theer some bugger had NICKED all her BITS. An I knew who wer goin to to get blamed for nickin em, yours truly. A pulled me keks up an wer art of that passage like a bullet from a gun.

A ran to r house owdin me trousers up wi mi ands, and charged inta kitchen. An of course me mam wer theer, gerrin dinner ready.

OH NO! A new what wer comin. Mam ant dun much schoolin, but she wer omnipresent like God, she alus new when ad bin up to no good. She asked mi why a wer art a breath, an why mi trousers were undone. This I thought this cud be a case were truth wer better than valor, so a telled her wor appened. Which resulted ina good hidin, and the usual threat of "wait till a tell ya dad".

The moral here, is before yer start messin wi wimin learn to fasten yer trouser buttons.

Chapter 2 Movin On Up. Startin School

That First Day

I suppose we all remember our first day at school, the fuss, mum chasing about making breakfast and ironing yer clothes so you looked smart. Then the long walk to school, and it wer a long walk. Nope not in our house, mi mum wer a cleaner darn at Canklow Ex Servicemen's Club n had gone to work before I gorup, mi dad wer in bed, bin on nights at Steelos. So the next door neighbour Mrs Ramsden took mi to school on mi first day. A dint mind cos Pat her daughter wer mi first love. I dint think nowt of Mum not being wi mi on that day, after all a wer all of 5 years old, old enough to look after misen, burit must av left a scar cos it still pains mi today 65 years later.

The infant years passed like the early years wi no major trauma, sept for a couple er feyts, usually wi girls, over who's ball it wer, or cos ad nicked their skippin rope to mek a lasso like Hopalong Cassidy, or ad tied one er em to school railins, an they wernt able to undo knots.

More about feyts later cos they seemed to appen a lot in my life.

The Junior School.

"Stick or the Sipper".

Movin on up to the Junior School. It wer time to find art what real life wer all about. It wer goin to get tougher, the rules became stricter, an the punishment fer breckin them rules wer goin to be swift an painful, resulting in "The Stick" or "The Slipper". Depending on which Teacher was presiding over the rule of Law.

My own personal preference (if there is such a thing when it comes to corporal punishment, wert slipper, cos it left no visible marks. Unlike the stick which made your fingers swell and glow red for hours, n if a went home wi bright Red fingers mi Mam knew ad ad stick an gin mi another good hidin cos ad ad stick.

I found out pretty quick how these, new to me, rules worked.

On mi first day in mi new class int Juniors, our teacher Mr Parkin explained how important it wer to look after school equipment, and any misuse of said equipment would result in the culprit being punished, seemed fair to me, not being a destructive type.

At which point a dropped mi pencil ont floor. As a bent darn to pick it up, a loud voice bellowed out **"you boy what's your Name"**. Well a looked round to see who he wer shoutin at. He wer lookin straight at me. **"Yes you boy, you wi the specs on"** that ad bi me then, "me sir", came a squeaky sound out of mi gob, "yes you" "John Brogan Sir" "Out front now" I meekly went to the front of the class.

"What did you just do Brogan" he asked. "A dropped mi pencil Sir". "And what did I say would happen to people who misuse school equipment". "They will be punished Sir". **"Right"**. He reached behind his desk and produced a long thin sorta walkin stick n started thrashin it up n darn in the air "hand out Brogan"."Burit wer an accident Sir". "Don't talk back at me Brogan, you can have another one for your cheek now. Hand out".

Ouch

I held mi hands out, screwed mi eyes tight shut, a herd this swishing noise an felt a burnin sensation on mi right hand, followed by another swish and burnin on mi left hand.

At this point a wer really hurtin an ready to cry, bura wer from Canklow a wernt goin to let him, or the class see mi cry. So a folded mi arms as tight as a cud, to try to stop the pain, an went an sat darn. When a gor home mi Mam wanted to know ar mi first day int Big school ad gone, a telled her a wernt over impressed and left it at that.

A went to bed that night an sobbed mi heart out. Did corporal punishment at 8 years old make mi a better person, NO. Did it give the teacher some kind of thrill, YES. Oh! an a found out later the Teacher was known as "Flogger Parkin" and I know why.

This wernt mi last brush wi corporal punishment, wait till yer hear abart the flyin chisel and the woodwork teacher, but as they allas sey, the first cut the deepest.

A Brush Wi Death

When we're growin up, we're told that your school days r the best
times of yer life. Well who ever tells yer that, r lyin. Cos it's the bits in
between yer school days, like Weekends and Holidis, that're best days
of yer life, and create the most memories, so here's some of mine.

It maybe because of mi Rose tinted glasses burrit never seemed to rain
int summer Holidis, n ifin it did, it went mostly un-noticed. Whatever
appened it never stopped yer from playin art.

A life threatenin incident appened to me in the middle of one
particularly hot dry summer. It wer one a them summers whent sun
seemed t shine every day.
After weeks of dry weather the level of the river Rother had dropped to
a mere stream, this caused the mud banks to dry up leaving a crust on
top of the mud. It actually looked like a Roman mosaic than a mud
bank.

To set the scene picture this.

At the bottom of ar street wer a field of meadow grass, and wild
flowers, which led down to the river Rother where Kingfishers sang in
the overhangin reeds, and salmon and trout swam, in its crystal clear
waters.

Wrong! The meadow was actually a rubbish tip where Council Dustbin
wagons dumped the stinking waste of all Rotherham, and due to the
industrial factories upstream, dumping every chemical, and poisonous
substance invented, into the river, the river Rother was the most
polluted river in Europe and nowt could live in it.

Anyway! back to mi tale.

Na no self-respecting 8 year old kid, and especially a Canklow kid, is going to resist the temptation to walk on this newly exposed land. That's when it append. Ad just got abart 10 foot from the grass bank, when the crust gave way.

Plunging me up to mi waist into a pool of thick slimy mud, that wer black as Ace o Spades and stunk to high heaven of every pollutant known to man. Now if that wernt bad enough. I wer goin to die. Drownin in stinking mud. An when yer resign yer sen to dyin, an ya think it can't ger eny worse. It does!

Some silly bugger gus n fetches mi mam (big mistake).

Mi Mam appears wi er turbin on her ead and a face like thunder, and carryin her best sweepin brush. Well bless her. She saves mi life, usin the sweepin brush handle to pull me art. But then proceeded to try an kill mi, by hittin mi wi said sweepin brush, every step of the way home.

Funny how some things stick in your mind.

It wernt allus Summer Holidis that wer special, Satdis and Sundis wer Special anall.

Typical Satdi in Canklow

That means tanner rush at the Essoldo.

The Essoldo Rotherham

Tanner Rush, So called because it cost a tanner or 6d, to go in. It were a good mornins entertainment. They pura film on, then a cartoon. At the Interval they had kids on the stage doin silly things. Singin, dancing n, a new craze called a Hula Hoop. All these kids on stage med great practice for mi pea shooter, dint half mek em jump when they got clouted wi a fast movin dried pea ont backside. After Interval came the Serial. This wer usually a Hopalong Cassidy Film, or Flash Gordon.

An it allus ended when somebody wer about to get killed off. Then on the screen it would say TO BE CONTINUED NEXT WEEK. That wer just to get you to gu back. But yer wer goin to gu back anyway. Cos ther wer no wear else to gu on Satdi morning.

The problem is if tha from Canklow thas probably shorta cash. The tanner t gerin int a problem. Mi mum ad gladly gimi that to get mi from under her feet.

Total so far 6d

It's the money to buy thi pop, n ice cream, oh n thee peas. Yes! thee peas. Oh! Come on how can ya gu to pictures wiart peas for thi pea shooter?

So Here's the Plan

First thing Satdi morning. Bora mi sisters pram. Shill not miss it cos shis only 3, an still in bed. Fill pram wi scrap metal, that I found sorta just lyin around, throughout the week. Then its darn to Boothies scrap yard on owd Sheffield road, to weigh scrap in for cash.Only got 2 Bob. Got ripped o by blokes on wayin scale cos am only 8 year owd and dunt know how the scales work.

Total now 2/6d

Then back home. To do some more recycling. Returnin pop bottles back to Co-op, for 3 pence each. (A call this recycling, cos the pop bottles am tekin back, are the same pop bottles, av just nicked from the back of the shop. Where they store em, after yer tek em back. Hence recyclin). **Grand Total 3/6d** Woo Hoo

Then it's off to pictures. After callin into indoor market for mi dried peas. Only Batchelors dried peas would do. They were more expensive but a perfect fit n dint get stuck in yer pea shooter. Once again enterprise wins the day..

21

Sundis a used to luv Sundis.

Sundis wer alus special. Yer did things on Sundis yer dint do on any other day of week. When a gorup mi dad would gi mi threpence to gu to Sundi School at St Luke's (threpence wer fer collection not fer me).

There wer sumat strange abart goin to Sundy School, cos me Mam n Dad wernt religious sort a people, but they were reyt pleased to see me go to Sundi School. When a kem back hom a noticed me Dad allus had a sorta silly grin on is face n mi Mam ad reyt red rosy cheeks. I dunt know wor they ad been doin but wor ever it wer, it med em both happy.

At twelve O,clock, mi Dad would bugger off t Ex Servicemen's club at bottom of r street, for a pint (or 2). While mam got Sundi dinner ready.

Dinner wer allus at 2 a clock sharp, not 5 ta or 5 past, an ifn yer wer late, yer dinner wer int dog.

Na there's a lot bin said abart Sundi dinner, but for any o them suthern Jessie's that might read this, this is how it shud be dun. Yorkshire puddin wi gravy on, fa starter (when a sey Yorkshire puddin a mean proper Yorkshire puddin, med in a great roastin tin. Not them fart arse little ant Bessie things. Then ya veg, n roast beef, n mash, n greens, for main. An then Yorkshire pud wi jam on fer puddin.(they call it a sweet or dessert darn sarth).

A strange thing Happened when a ad mi sundi dinner a bekem a vegitarian. Mi Mother telled mi a dint like meat. I dint know how she knew a dint like meat.

22

You see ad never ad chance to taste it. Bur if ya can't trust yer Mam who can yer trust?

Na ano that kids from Canklow maybe a bit rough round edges, but you'd never leave the dinner table wiart askin "please may I leave the table" if yer dint ask yer wer lynin yer sen up for a flea in thi ear.

After dinner it wer art to play, while mi dad ad a nap. Wor ever he'd bin doin int mornin, med him tired int afternoon. Well we've ad us dinner (it's not lunch it's dinner). We would play fer a couple of hours. An then back home fer tea. First question yer ask when yer get thru door is, " mam wots fer tea". Ya know what the answer, is before yer ask the question, " shit wi sugar on" allus same answer, don't know why I asked.

Am hoping we've got visitors fa tea. Cos me mam try's t be posh when we have Visitor's. We have real tinned salmon. Instead of the usual bread an jam.

Na me mam wer magic wi salmon, she'd open a 2oz tin of John West salmon, mix it up wi a big lump of Stork margarine into a paste. She'd spread it onto bread, then she'd scrape it all off again. By doin this she could mek the smallest tin feed six people, n have enough left fer mi dads snap on Mondi. After salmon sandwiches we'd ave a tin a fruit cocktail wi tinned Carnation milk, n bread n Stork margarine.

After tea it werr bath time. I allus had a bath on Sundi even if a dint need one.

We wer lucky we had a bath upstairs, n hot watter on tap. Not like me aunt Clara at number 40. She had a black lead range to heat watter, an ad to bring a tin bath from outside, inta kitchen to get bathed in.

23

It were or reyt fer mi Uncle Herb, his watter wer pipin ot, cos he wer first in. Then it wer mi Aunt Clara's turn. Then mi cousins Celia, then our Gay. When it wer ar Bernard's turn, watter wer clap cold. Cos he wer youngest and number 5 int queue.

A wer a bit jealous really cos they could use their tin bath art side ont back yard an use it as a paddlin pool int summer.
A luxury we had beside the upstairs bathroom, was a detached Toilet. Yes detached. I know some of the people reading this may not agree with me about this being a luxury.
But look at it from my point of view. Once, as a 7 year old, I had been on a fishing trip wi mi Dad and Uncle Vince Copley to a place called Salters Lode on the old Bedford River.

We stayed in what could loosely be described as a Guest House. Set on the river bank. The "Guest House" had no running water. We had to fetch it from a nearby well, No electricity the light was provided via gas mantles, that popped a banged. Each time scaring me to death, and a few candles. The toilet like ours, was detached and was located at the bottom of the long garden.

My first visit was my last.

Compare this to our luxury toilet.

Ours had no door lock, but it had a sneck, so to ensure privacy, you learned to whistle. You would find out that most people who lived on Castle Avenue could whistle better than Ronnie Renalde.

Theirs dint even av a door.

Ours had neat squares of the Rotherham Advertises on a hook behind the door. You can have a read, catching up on the local news, or do a crossword before you er, recycled the paper, if you know what I mean.

Theirs dint have a door, so no hook, no paper.

Ours had a chain and a cistern. You could flush away the paper, that had been on the hook. that was behind the door.

Theirs dint have a cistern an no runnin water, so you wernt able to flush away the paper, that wasn't on the hook, because there was no bloody door.

Our toilet had a seat that was made of beautifully carved wood. That perfectly fitted the shape of your bum.

25

Theirs was a plank of wood. Wi 2 holes cut in it, a big hole for big bums, and a little hole for, yes, little bums. And underneath the plank. No drainage. The smell was? Well, al leave that to your imagination.

Now you tell that ours wasn't luxurious.

Praise Where its Due

Before I go on to the next bit I would like to give mi Mam and Dad a bit of praise. Mi Dad worked long hours in the steelworks. So he could buy us nice things. I don't know what he did exactly. But whatever it wer, he often worked seven days a week doin it. Mi Mam on the other hand had two part time jobs an did all the house work to a strict routine. Mundis wer wesh day, Tuesdis Ironin an purin weshin away, Wensdis, Scrub front an back steps wi pumice stone. Clean winders and polish winder sills wi Red Cardinal, sweep causeway. Thursdi, Bake bread and cakes, oh that smell hmmmm. Fridis, wer market day so Mam goes shoppin.

A allus remember as a kid, of about 8 oh and n half, the half wer important when yer wer young. Mundi being wesh day. Mi Mum like everybody else ont street did all their weshin on Mundy. An if it wernt rainin, it wer hung ont line to dry. They used an energy savin invention back then, called wind, n sun.

Every month, or so, mi Mum would wesh mi short trousers. This would mean a would av to wear mi other pair of trousers, "mi best trousers". I hated it cos shi wunt let mi play art in mi best trousers. Worst of all shi med mi empty mi pockets before shi weshed mi mucky trousers. Na a know this wunt be hard for modern kids, mobile phone and headphones, job done.

Not me. Here goes

Time to empty mi pockets:- Back pocket, Catapult, Flashlamp, Air gun pellets, Dirty hankie, Three half pennies and mi Swiss army knife. Front pockets, Pet Mouse, 6 Marbles, 5 Conkers, Box of Matches, Piece of String, Part sucked Gob Stopper and some chewed chewing gum a wer saving for later. A wer allus glad to get mi old trousers back. Cos mi Mam ad sewed all the pockets up on mi new trousers so a wernt able to fill em wi rubbish. Rubbish! I ask yer? This wern't rubbish. These wer everyday essentials.

Mi First Holidi

It ad be abart 1954. Wi wer one o the first families on the street to own
a motor car. A Grey Morris 1000, registration MFS 509.

It's funny how I can remember this registration, but can't remember the
registration of my car present car, parked outside. A went on mi first
proper Summer Hollidi that a could remember. Mi big brother ar Pete
dint gu cos he wer courtin n a don't know who had mi little sister but
she wernt wi us.

Mi Dad drove us all the way to the Lake District. It wer a long way. No
motorways in them days. Wi stayed at a place called Askam- in- Furness, with
mi Aunt Edie and Uncle Jack.

Yes another Aunt an Uncle, burra dint call on this one at Whitsuntide.

MFS 509

Askam-in-Furness wer small seaside village that made Canklow look like the Big City. It consisted of just 2 rows of owd houses, and was separated from the beach by a large allotment. The allotment had a pathway through it, that led down to the said beach.

I mention the pathway because it became the focus of the holiday and created a love for dogs that has never ceased.

Because of its isolated location, an the fact mi mam n dad wer busy doin other things. I was let loose, sorry, allowed to do my own thing durin the day. Right, first thing darn to the beach, it wernt far, you could see it from where we were stayin.

The Path to Freedom

All a had to do was follow the pathway straight darn to beach. All went well till I got close to the allotment. Blockin the path were a load great big birds, skawkin an hissin an flappin there wings up an darn as if they owned the place. I later found out they wer called geese. Na am not one fer backin darn in an argument but the odds wer stacked against mi. The wer a lot more of them than ther wer me. An a wernt armed, no bow an arrow, no Bowie knife, nowt.

Na a considered misen a City Kid comin from Rotherham, and dint know much abart animals and country life. The most I knew abart animals wer the bantams n rabbits that mi Aunt Clara kept on her back yard.

A turned round an wer about to run like hell, when this snarling black and white dog appeared from no weer. A thought O shit! am goin to be attacked by these bloody big birds, an savaged by a dog.

Am goin to die "again" an Mi mam al kill mi if mi trousers get ripped.

Back Off

The dog ran streyt past mi barkin like mad, he chased all the geese away an then kem back waggin his tail. He escorted me to the beach and stayed wi mi till a went back. The dog, a Border Collie called Jack. Was my constant companion on that Hollidi. The geese never bothered me agean, and Jack gave me a lifelong trust in dogs. **That's more than a can say for a lot of humans av met.**

This chance meeting with a four legged friend led to me owning my own dog.

A Present Surprise, Tinged with Tragedy.

One day on returning home from school, mi Dad sed "close thi eyes av got thee a present". A thought! It's not mi Birthday, an its no were near

Christmas, an a ant asked or owt new lately .

Ah well al tek a chance. A closed mi eyes an mi Dad led mi through to the front room. He ses "right open em". A removed mi hands from mi eyes, and there before me was a large closed cardboard box. "Go on open it " mi Dad sed.

Not bein used to surprises, especially from mi Dad. I used extreme caution openin the box. When a gorit open a peered inside an gora shock, in the darkness of the box, there wer sumat peerin back at mi. "Go on" mi Dad ses "pick it up". A reached timidly into the box, only to be greeted by a set of needle like teeth."Oh come here" mi dad ses, he reaches into the box, and produces the cutest little puppy ad ever seen."Here thy are it's thine" and hands it over to me. "Mine !" "Yes it's yours to keep" ses Dad. This wer the happiest day of my 10 years of life. Never ad a bin gin such a precious and beautiful present.

After a gor over the shock and surprise, a picked up mi puppy an sed "a think al call it Lassie after that dog on TV. "That could cause thee a problem" ses mi dad. "Why?" kem my reply. "Cos Lassie is a girl dog, n your's is a boy dog". Warabout Rin Tin Tin then". "No." ses mi Dad" that's a name for an Alsatian". "A know al call it Laddie", "spot on ses mi Dad".

So Laddie it wer.

Now you need the rules of ownin a dog, and a promise from you, of keepin them rules." Mi Dad sed. In a serious voice, so that a new he meant it. "Do you promise me. You will look after Laddie at all times. Train him to be obedient, make sure he's house trained. Feed and water him properly, an tek him for plenty of walks"." Course I will Dad, a promise". "It wer like gerin married, a thought. Right Laddies all yours.

I can't wait to tell all mi mates av gora dog of mi own.

Remeberin mi promise to mi Dad.The trainin started almost straight away.

Mi Dad sed mi puppy wer a Pedigree Mongrel. Ad never heard of that breed before. But to me he looked like a Labrador Border Collie cross. Yer see I'm not as green as am cabbage lookin. Laddie wer as Black as Ace of Spades like a Labrador wi a White diamond shaped patch on his chest like a Border Collie.

Gerin him house trained wer a pain. Lots of piles of poo to pick up. Yuk. And thousands of little puddles to mop up.
His trainin wer goin a treat. I taught him to sit,stay, lie-down. all on my command, I even taught him to give me a paw before he ad a meal.
I was still havin trouble gerin him"come to heal" I think it was because he wer part Border Collie and liked exlporin. So he pretended to be deaf and ignored me. But we wer gerin theer, slowly but surly.
After six months wid become inseparable. Weer I went. Laddie went. Except school of corse.

One Sundi mornin a wok up early as ad planned campin trip into Canklow woods. A looked down the side of mi bed and noticed Laddie wernt theer. A thought it strange cos he never went down stairs before me, bur a thought na more about it. When a went downstairs into the kitchen.A wer surprised to see that mi Mam an Dad wer already up an dressed. Strange I thought, they usually av a mornin in bed on Sundi.

As a passed em on the way to the pantry, a sed "wher's Laddie"? To no one in particular.Mi Dad ses "sit down our John av got sumat to tell thi". The term "our John" wer only used when a wer in trouble or it wer sumat serious.

Na av seen mi Dads face change many time throughout mi life. Av seen his happy face, his angry face, his pissed out of his head face. But looking at him in the dawn light, I saw a face ad never seen before. His face wer ashen grey and he looked as though he ad bin up all night. A sat next to him at the kitchen table, tryin to work out why he looked so different. It wer then he sed "John there's been a terrible accident involving Laddie". "He's all reyt int he" a sed. No he was hit by a car on Canklow road and died from his injuries.

A bomb went off in mi head, a started swearin at mi dad. Sumat ad never done before in mi life. A wer cryin, an sobbin. A started punching him anywhere I could, an he just sat there and took it. I had completely lost it, I was inconsolable. My Dad held me tightly an cried with me. In a show of affection that he'd never ever given me before in my life. This was the first time I had suffered the loss of someone or something so close to me. Who was mine. Who loved me as much as I loved him.

It was a terrible introduction to death. Not only to death, but the death of a loved one. It wernt like the movies, or a game of Cowboys and Indians. It wer real and painful and it hurt like hell.

When I eventually settled down. My dad explained what happened that night. It was a Saturday night, and my Mum decided to go and meet my Dad, when he came out of the Club at the bottom of our street. She decided to take Laddie with her for company and because she did not want to wake me to get Laddies lead from my bedroom, she decided to make him walk to heal. Which he had now mastered. When she got to the bottom of the street she saw my Dad talking to some mates. Laddie heard my Dads voice and made a dash towards him, straight into the path of a car. killing Laddie instantly.

We buried Laddie on my Dads allotment, so that I could visit him any time I wanted. I found it hard to forgive my Mother for the hurt caused. **Even now, I don't really know if I ever did?**

The Club Trip, Pop, Crisps and Sick bags

For many kids, me included, the club day trip wer as near as you got to an annual holiday. Local working men's clubs organised these trips, and parents paid subscriptions throughout the year. It wasn't unusual to go more than one. My typical trips wer Albion Road Club, Trades and Labour Club and of course my favourite Canklow Ex Servicemen's Club. The excitement walkin darn Castle Avenue to see coaches lined up along Canklow Road as far as young lads eyes could see. It dint matter weer you wer off to, you wer leavin the noisy, polluted and smoke blackened town n goin to seaside. For each club trip mi Mam alus med an effort to dress us respectable. An even she, like most o women, glammed her sen up a bit. She'd av curlers in her hair covered wi an head scarf, nora turban like she usually wore, n when we arrived at sea side, all women would dash into ladies Loo. Whip off their scarves, out wi rollers, an on wi mek up.

All Aboard for The Club Trip

When they kem art ya could hardly recognise em. An mi Dad sed toilets smelt like a tarts bedroom wharever one o them wer.

As soon as wi set off it started, "The Singin". All the owd war songs that soldiers used to sing. All the stuff off the radio. Mi own personal favourite " How much is that doggy in the window" don't worry if ya ant heard it, they sang loads a songs ad never heard. Singin usually lasted allway theer, and back, except fer when we stopped at a pub half way. So men could av a pint n women could ave a wee. Which took some time considerin there wer usuall only one Ladies Loo for 20 bus loads of women.

On the way to seaside club stewards would come round wi free pop n crisps, which when you'r not used ta been gin stuff fer free, you tend to get a bit greedy hence the need for sick bags. Also while on the journey the stewards presented each and every kid with a little brown envelope, and usually contained 5 brand new, never bin used Two Bob pieces. Yes ad Ten Bob, my Ten Bob to spend on owt a wanted. Christmas forget Christmas. A wer rich a felt like a millionaire.

Ad already planned wora wer goin to spend it on. On this occasion as we wer goin to Cleethorpes a would be buyin sum binoculars'. So a cud see the sea. You'll know wora mean if yerv ever bin to Cleethorpes. If we'd bin going to Brid ad av bought a knife, it wer alus hard choosin a knife, wer it to be a sheaf Knife wi a long blade so a cud play stretch, or an Army knife, for when a wer campin in Canklow woods. Tough decisions when yer only 8 years owd.

While were talkin about knives, a wer lookin at one o them Army knives, n tryin to work art what all the blades wer for, it had so many. Well ad worked em all art except one. It wer like a long spike wi a bend in it. Now ther's only one person in the World that knows the answer to everything, yer Dad.

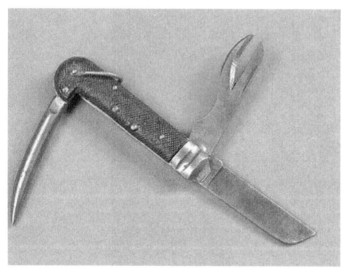

Dad Whats This Bent Spike For?

Dad whats this spike thing on mi Army knife for? "Its for gerrin Boy Scouts art horses hooves", na a know mi Dad dunt tell lies but sometimes he meks mi wonder.

Durin the day mi Mam would feed us fish n chips washed down wi a milk shake, n we'd have some candy floss, the occasional ice cream, some rock, then kali and liquorice. Then we'd go on the beach for an hour. Mi Dad n his mates went to pub instead of goin on beach. Mi Dad said he dint like sand.

Then it wud bi onto funfair. To go on the Big Dipper an Waltzer before gerrin onto bus back home.

Now the journey goin home wer different to goin. The singin carried on, but not as loud. And we ad to stop loads a times. All men would dash art n all line up along hedge bottom, a dint know what they wer doin, but they seemed happier each time they got back on.

It wer a lot quieter goin back, except for the kids being sick cus they'd stuffed ther sens wi rubish, that's what mi Mam sed.

Me sick? Na am from Yorkshire waynt part wi nowt. Allus slept well after a trip to Seaside.

Who's the kid wi specs on? Oh that'd bi me.

Games Kids played and Mrs Ackroyd

Hiddy wer mi favourite game. Also known as Hide and Seek to Posh Ki
The Street outside your house wer for playing on. No need to worry
about cars, nobody ad got one. Except mi Dad an he wer allus at work
Then there wer the side field. I don't know why they called it Side
Field. A guess that it wer cos where at the side of the houses. This
is where most of the lads played Twenty aside football or cricket Hiddi
wernt the only game wi played. So here's some others.

Now to keep the Politically Correct, Health and Saftey, Equal
Oportunities, Sexual Equaalities, Equal Rights, Friends of The Earth,
etc. etc. etc. Brigades happy. I wiould like to put out this statement.

"This is not a complete list of games that were available. Other games were equally popular and could be played instead. The games mentioned were open to all sexual orientations to participate in. No preferance was allocated in the case of gender, colour, creed or age. There may have been on occassions mostly in ball games where the owner of the equipment overuled decisions made. The one rule that the above assosiations may find causes some offence is "The Fatest Kid wer allways int Goal". Well you will just av to suck it up baby. That was the rule"

Unlike todays kids, where you have to drag them, kicking and screaming. First to get them to release their grip off the X Box, and then to get them past the front door. We were the exact oposite. Your Mother would usually shout for you to come in as dusk approched. Which you would tottaly ignore, prettending you dint hear her. Next she would put in a personal appearence. Grab you by the lughole, drag you down the side passage and in through the back door. Job done. How things have changed.

Right here is the list of games, in no particular order. I am listing the games in name only and not including the rules. This is because the rules were often open to interpritation. Often causing confrontation and ending in some cases in. Yes you have guessed it. A FEYT.

As I said previously this is not a complete list. It just gives you an idea why we wer never in.

The List
Kick Can, Hopscotch, Whip and Top, Kiss Catch, British Bulldog, Finger Thumb A Dumb, Hot Rice, Tiggy and Tiggy Off The Ground, Skipping. Farmer Farmer.

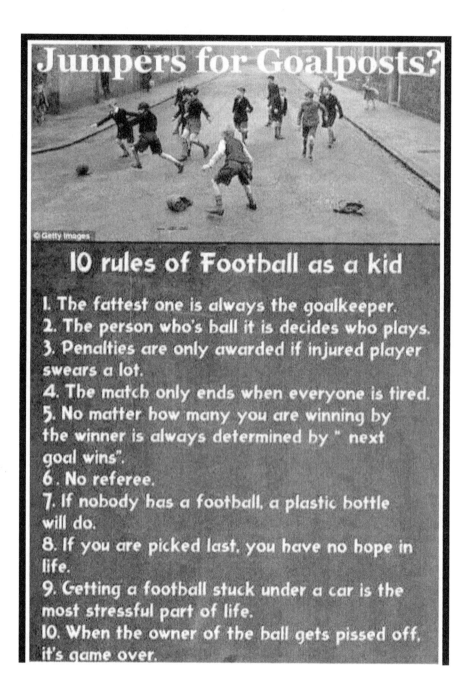

Jumpers for Goalposts?

© Getty Images

10 rules of Football as a kid

1. The fattest one is always the goalkeeper.
2. The person who's ball it is decides who plays.
3. Penalties are only awarded if injured player swears a lot.
4. The match only ends when everyone is tired.
5. No matter how many you are winning by the winner is always determined by " next goal wins".
6. No referee.
7. If nobody has a football, a plastic bottle will do.
8. If you are picked last, you have no hope in life.
9. Getting a football stuck under a car is the most stressful part of life.
10. When the owner of the ball gets pissed off, it's game over.

At last Sumat a wer good at.

Av already confessed to bein useless at sport. Burra a wer reyt good at hiddy. A wer that good at gerrin hiddid that sometimes, all the other kids ad gone in fer their Tea an I wer still hidin.

It wer during a game of hiddy that a met Mrs Ackroyd. Mrs Ackroyd lived about five doors above us on Castle Ave. Ad never seen her, but mi Mam described her as a widder woman, worever that wer. Her garden wer like a jungle, overgrown wi trees, an plants, an weeds four foot tall. Perfect for gerin hiddid in.

One day I was just gerrin hiddid in her garden. When this woman suddenly appeared from no wear, n shouted "What you up to?" well a spun round. An theer she wer. Mrs Ackroyd.

She wer dressed all in Black, tatty mucky clothes. She stunk awful, like the men's urinals, on Canklow playing field.

Thinkin on mi feet, an as quick as a flash. A ses " am just admirin this beautiful purple flower on this tree.

"Oh! that's a Sumac" she says. Then continues to give me the life history, of a bloody tree. After which she thrusts a small tree into my hand an says "here you are you can grow your very own Sumac."

Well not only do I not like sport I din't like gardening either. Reason being, mi Dad ad a great big allotment. Guess which one of his three kids had to do all the watterin an weedin? No it wasn't Kathryn. Cos she wes a girl. No it wernt Peter. Cos mi Mam sed it would make his hands rough". Yes it wer me, an I I hated it.

I see A Golden Opportunity Arise.

Mi Dad loved his gardenin, so a thought here's a chance to ger in his good books. A went round home, tree in hand, found mi Dad in his greenhouse, and proudly presented him wi mi newly acquired tree.

Now a wer just goin to educate him wi all the knowledge I had just gained, about the Sumac Tree. When he took one look at this pretty little tree an ses. "What the Bloody Hell has tha brought this for, does tha know wharit is"?

Well a wer just about to tell him that, wernt a.

He ses " it's a bloody Sumac, a bloody Sumac". "Plant this an in a couple of years it'll av spread all over the bloody garden an you can't stop it, and promptly chucked it in weed bin. End of Sumac,

Sometimes, just sometimes, I suspected that mi Dad over reacts in certain situations, and this was one of them. How could such a beautiful flowering tree be so troublesome.Well once again my Dad was proved right.

I recently went on a nostalgic trip down memory lane. I went through Canklow and parked on what was left of Castle Avenue. The street was still there, but the houses had gone. Where our house used to be was a small pile of bricks n rubble.

And what of Mrs Ackroyds house. Well just rubble like ours. except with a bloody great big Sumac Tree growing through it. Even the Bulldozer could not stop it 60 years later.

Dad I apologise, once again you wer right.

Things We Did For Fun.

Swimmin A Know a sed a dint like Sport, but swimming wer different.Swimmin wernt a sport. It wer Fun, an sport int Fun.

Old Baths Main Street
Rotherham
Here is A Little Quiz

Q: Who was the first person to swim the English Channel ?

A: Captain Matthew Webb. Most people know this because it said so on a box of matches.

Q: Who wer second person to swim the English Channel?

A: William Thomas Burgess in 1911. They always say nobody remembers the person who comes second in an event.

**So why is this mans achievement so important. Because he wer
from Rotherham that's why.**

To celebrate this achievement, a bonze bust were made of him, and
placed on show at the entrance to the swimmin baths. I mention this,
because every kid who went to the baths, and some grown ups too, used
to rub his nose wi their rolled up towel as they went in. This wer to
bring em luck, and hopefully not to drown. It also resulted, over the
years as a well patinaed dark bronze bust with a almost Golden nose.

Would I Sink or Swim?

A learned to swim wen a wer int Junior School. Swimmin lessons wer
compulsory, but yer dint av to force mi to go to this lesson. It wer a
long walk to the Baths, especially if it wer cold or rainin, an worse if it
wer doin both at the same time.

The Bloke who taught us to swim, wernt a teacher, he wer just a man
that worked at the baths. He wer called Mr. Norton, an he wer cruel.

Mr Norton showed you what to do wi yer arms an hands, and then
showed yer what to do wi yer legs n feet. Na this wer easy for him cos
he wer stood ont side of pool fully dressed. Not bobbin up and darn like

corks artra bottle, gaspin for breath every time yer managed to get yer gob arta watter.

The First Challenge

Your first challenge when you'd learnt the arm strokes, and the leg strokes, wer to get them to work together. When you'd achieved this and had got some semblance of a swimmin stroke, you would attempt to swim a width of the pool. Not a length that wer a different challenge, one tha you got a certificate for.

When you wer first learnin to swim, you'd all gather in shallow end and cling on to the side of the pool. Now when a say the shallow end, it wernt that shallow when you are only 3 foot 6 tall an the waters 4 foot deep.

Now this is where Mr. Norton first shows his cruel streak.

A width of the pool, might not sound far. A mean it's only 12 n half yards. Which it int far for most people. But put yer sen in my shoes. Me three foot six in four foot of watter, short sighted, can only just see mi hand in front o mi face, ni mind other side of the pool, cos am not allowed to wear mi specs.

Reyt it's my turn to try n swim a width.

Push off from t side, swim-splash-dog paddle-drown-spit watter out. More or less in that order. When it gets to the drown bit, Mr Norton comes to the rescue. Now remember, he's not in the watter, he's stood on side fully clothed. So how does he rescue mi. Wi a bloody gret long barge pole, that he has specially for these kind of occasions.

Yer supposed to be swimmin in it, not drinkin it.

Am half way across the pool, when he shouts grab the pole. The pole wer about twelve foot long, and he tapped mi ont ead wi it, to let mi know weer it wer, cos ad no chance of bein able to see it wi art mi specs on. A med a grab at the pole an missed. A went under watter an come back up splutterin an coughin. Grab the bloody pole. Ya could tell he wernt a teacher, teachers dint ever swear. Well a went to grab the pole, burit wer to far in front o mi. So under a went agean, then back up an grab, an miss cos he'd moved it. Wi all this happenin ad not noticed ad actually reached the other side of the pool.

Congratulation lad, thas just swum thee first half length, well in a fashion.

Well the crafty bugger. He knew wari wer doin all the time, an mi swimmin went from strength to strength. Mi half length wer follower quickly by the full length mi first certificate, 16 length a quarter of a mile, half a mile, and a mile and finally mi life savin. For which a got a certificate n a badge for mi Mam to sew on to mi swimmin trunks.

A Hard Choice for A Yorksher Kid

When it came to swimmin and the other hobbies I had at the time. It wer always a hard choice of which would be a priority. The dilemma was this. School finished at 4 o'clock. So choices wer. Train Spottin or Swimmin. To go swimmin cost money.

So if ad got no money it wer easy. At 4 o clock ad set off to run the mile and a half darn to Masborough Station to see the Waverley, London to Edinburgh Train pass through. More on Train spottin later.

But if ad got some cash it would be straight down to the New Baths on Sheffield Road.

The New Baths wer better than the Old Baths not just because they wer newer. But because the wer bigger an deeper and ad a 5 metre high divin platform.

Yet another Dilemma. The Baths had hourly sessions that started on the hour. So here's the dilemma. The session that starts at 4 o'clock cost 4d to go in. The session at 5 o'clock rose to 6d to go in.

ROTHERHAM CORPORATION
SUPER
SWIMMING BATH
AND
DIVING POOL

SHEFFIELD ROAD ——— ROTHERHAM

Telephone 1018

SUMMER SEASON
OPEN FOR MIXED BATHING AT ALL TIMES.

MONDAY to SATURDAY ...... 7 a.m. to 10 p.m.
SUNDAYS .... 7 a.m. to 10 a.m.

ADULTS 6d.   CHILDREN 4d. after 5 p.m.
And Sunday Morning, Children 6d.

Spectators are admitted to CAFE at a charge of 4d. per head (including
Light Refreshment).

MAIN STREET BATHS ARE ALSO OPEN DAILY for SWIMMING,
SLIPPER, & TURKISH BATHS. For particulars, apply at Main St. Baths.

Swim your way to Health and Happiness

F. A. STEVENS,
Baths Superintendent.

If I leave school at 4 o'clock an a run like hell a can get to the baths for
10 past four pay mi fourpence, get changed an in the water for quarter

past four. Or wait till the 5 o'clock session and pay sixpence but get mi full hour. "What would you do"?

What did I do? As mi dad allus sed "never spend a bob weer a tanner al do". It wer allus the four o clock session fer me.
Finally on the subject of swimmin,

A Warning!

An event that happened at one of the sessions might be worth a mention as a warnin to other kids out there. Like they say on telly "Don't Try This At Home". It wer at one of these sessions that I had an amazin escape. We dint go to the sessions to train or do owt serious, it wer to have a laugh and muck abart. The divin platform I mentioned earlier, being the centre for our entertainment.

Don't Look Darn

The height of this platform wer a bit disconcerting. If you stood on the edge and looked down the 5 metre drop into 3 of metres water, it wer a long, long way down.

The platform consisted of a lower springboard, set a metre higher than the pool. This wer great for doin somersaults and the like. A second springboard set 3 meters above the pool. This wer for proper divin, not for amatures. The third level wer set a 5 meters above the pool, an it wer just a wide platform.

This wer a favorite for us kids. It wer so high that you wer up near the roof. So to avert any attack of nerves, or be overcome by fear, we used to stand reyt at the back of the board, start runnin as fast as we cud, so fast you wernt able to stop. Then tek a leap of faith into the unknown.

53

This wer a great thrill and yer could feel yer belly flutterin like it wer full of butterflies.

Do Not Try This At Home.

Na ad done this hundreds, if not millions of times. All of which ended successfully, meenin a dint drown. That was until one particular day, a climbed up the steps up to the top block, rested mi bum on the rail at the rear of the board, took a deep breath, then launched mi sen forward goin like a train, an off into space a went.

When yer in flight, its such a long way down, you have time to ponder a little. Well in this particular case, I wer given sumat to ponder abart.

It went sumat like "whats that bloke doin swimmin under water" then "whats he doin swimmin across my path" followed by "OH NO HE'S COMIN UP FER BREATH". At this stage you're committed to your fight path and can't change it.

He's comin up I'm goin down, then bang a landed on top of his ead just as it popped outa the water, shatterin mi heal bone, before even touching the water. I just sort of fell off his head into the pool.

Na a know you will be concerned, and want to know what happened to the poor bloke a landed on. Well am sorry you will have to guess cos I don't know I wer off to hospital to get mended.

So please kids. Always look to see what you are goin to land on before you tek to the skies.

Train Spottin

That bloke Danny Boyle took credit as the Director of the film Train Spotting burit wer us kids that invented the hobby of Train Spottin. Na yer might wat to go on to the next topic if yer not interested in steam trains, or how you can visit major cities for a penny return. But please read the bit where we beat the Germans to a World Record and still hold today.

Every hobby in the 50s and 60s seemed to involve some sort of outdoors activity. Be it on your own street, or somewhere more exotic like Doncaster, York or even Crewe.

I mention these places cos they wer special.

If ya wonderin why places such as these wer special, its cos they wer Railway Stations on the main London to Scotland rail links. An if yer wer a train spotter, these wer the places weer you might see the rare steam engines of the day.

Na us from Yorksher, are sometimes looked on by the folks from outside Gods county, as bein a bit slow. So here's sumat to shuram up.

On July 3,1938, the mighty Mallard was recorded as reaching the awe-inspiring speed of 126mph on the East Coast Main Line, breaking the existing German record of 124mph set in 1936. It wer built in Doncaster an it brok the world speed record in Yorksher.

So! Next time a German nicks yer Sunbed, it might bi worth while remindin him of this fact. An it still stands to this day. Back to Mi Train Spottin.

To train spot yer dint need much equipment. A Biro an book for train spotters. The books had all the details and engine numbers of the trains of a particular region of the country. You could get the books from big newsagents. They were written by a bloke called Ian Allen. A don't know weer he gor all the numbers of the engines from burit wernt my problem.

Wi pen and book at the ready, all you needed wer some trains to spot.

You may have noticed if yerv seen a train. There's a number on the side of the engine just below the drivers window. Each of these numbers relates to that one engine. No two engines have the same number. The idea is to record the number an then underline the correspondin number in Ian Allens book. This shows that you've seen or "spotted" that particular engine.

Hi Tech it's Not. I know it dunt sound very excitin, burit wer cheap to do an it got you out the house.

The Excitin Bit Wer Gerin to See the Engine's

Let me explain.

Rotherham wer a bit of a backwater when it came to trains. Wi one exception, the 4.20 pm Waverley Express, London to Edinburgh. This train came through Rotherham Masbro station, every week day. It was usually pulled by some of the more famous steam engines of the day.To get to see the Waverley. Meant a mile and half mad dash from South Grove School to The Coronation Bridge to get the best view of the engine. That Chis Bannister chap ad got nowt on our gang. Chargin through Rotherham like a heard o bulls, just to see a train.

As a said before to see best engines you ad got to go to the bigger more popular stations.

That would cost Money. Summat we dint have much of. So how do you get to these stations. First buy a Platform Ticket for a Penny. From machine in the ticket office.

This allowed you on to the platform.

The real purpose of the ticket was allow you the chance to say good by to your friends or family, who wer leavin on a train.

That's not what it allowed us to do. No. To us it wer a "Ticket to Ride"

Buy the ticket. Try to attach yourself close behind a couple or a family as you pass the Ticket Inspector, show him your ticket.

Once on the platform, you will have checked the timetable earlier, and know what trains were arriving, and also there destinations. So it was just a matter of choosing where you wanted to go, and wait for the train to arrive.

On the arrival of your chosen train, you would try to and a coach without a corridor. This would alleviate any need to keep an eye out for the guard. And off you would go, the world was your onion. Birmingham, Crewe, Doncaster, York. After a day of fun an train spottin at one of these exotic locations, and as you were not leaving the station platform. No one new were there. The return journey was to simply catch a train back home, making sure that you returned to the same station as you originated from. This was because you had to hand your platform ticket in the ticket Inspector on leaving the station,, and the ticket was only valid for that particular station.

A penny well spent.

Question. What Do Five Kids Make? Answer. A Gang.

Five Become Sailors *almost*

Comin to the end of mi Junior school years it wer time to move on an leave mi lovely teacher Flogger Parkin behind.

In my last term I read a book called Swallows and Amazons by a chap called Arthur Ransome.

It wer about a posh rich family from darn south, who took their family to the Lake District to dodge the bombs that Adolf kept sendin em. What fascinated me about this book, was that the kids of the family used a boat to go sailin round a lake, and formed a gang called the Swallows, and they ad feyts against another gang called the Amazons.

Now I had a group of regular pals, but we wer not classed as a gang cos we dint av a name. So I suggested to Chris Bell that we ought to have a gang name and an official Gang Leader. He agreed and a meetin wer arranged in Chris's Granddads garden shed, soon to become our gang hut.

It was agreed that Chris was to be leader, as we wer usin his granddads hut. I wer to become second in command, as I wer the eldest. Alan and John Senior and Martin Melia wer the subordinates.

Gang formed. It was now time to choose a name for the gang. My choice after readin Swallows n Amazons was The Chain an Anchor Gang. This was met with all round approval. So we wer now officially The Chain an Anchor Gang.

While at this meetin I explained how much fun the kids in Swallows and Amazons had avin a boat, and how good it would be if we had a boat to play in over the coming school holidis. This was also greeted with noddin heads all round.

Chris sed his Granddad ad some spare planks of wood behind the shed that we could use. I sed a could draw some plans to work to. We had all the tools we needed in the shed. So boat building here we come.

Plans drawn up on a page out of my school book. Lets begin to build our boat. **Planks, saws, hammers, nails at the ready. Build!**

We reckoned we should be finished by dinner time and would have all afternoon to go sailin.

That's when the first minor problem occurred. Where we wer goin to sail our boat? The River Rother was a no go. It flowed too fast and it wer rancid.

Ulley Reservoir wer next choice. But that wer five mile away and has we ant gora trailer wid av to carry the boat all the way.

Then we realised another tiny problem. The gang hut was on a raised piece of land 30 foot above the street, and the street wer on top of a bloody great big hill. This made us about 300 feet above sea level. Bein on top of a big hill int good for sailin.

But first we had a major problem to overcome. The planks we wer usin wer a bit rotten and full of knots, an every time you knocked a nail in a knot would fall out leavin behind a great big hole.

Na we knew boats dint sail well wi holes in em. Look war appened to the Titanic.

We soon realised that these little problems, could mount up and cause, a Big problem.

Time for a rethink.

Chris ses lets build a trolley instead. Great idea. Na that's why he wer made leader.

Pram wheels sorted, axles sorted, brand new trolley made. Job done. Now the Bloody great big hill that wer causin a problem, suddenly became useful.

Better Than Sailin

Ah well! It just wern't meant for us to become Swallows an Amazons, but our gang had just as much fun as those Posh kids in the book.

Winters Comin Time For Sledgin an Slidin

No matter what the month or whatever the weather, mi bedroom winder wer never completely closed. Even through the worst of the weather It stayed open.

As a kid winter wer one of me favourite season cos a loved sledgin and slidin.

Once ad got Christmas out of the way thoughts turned to snow.

Mi bedroom winder wer level with our detached toilet roof. This became my focus durin January. The roof was perfect for seein if it ad bin snowin int night and ar deep it wer.

No central heating and no double glazing, meant that the winder got covered in frost, not only on outside, but on the inside too. Yer wernt able to see a thing through it. The gap in the window was the only way a could see if it ad been snowin. Ad probably check four or five times in a night.

No wonder a wer alus knackered at school in January.

What do ya mean Mam! "I can't play out in that" Theer's only a couple o inches.

When The Snow Arrives, Its Time To Go Sledgin.

Livin on at the top of a hill wer great if yer loved sledging, or mekin slides. Old folk dint like. Burits different if you'r only a kid.

Na to go sledging yer first need a Sledge.

This is where mi Dads job comes in handy.He worked as a pipe fitter at Steelos. This gave him access to the tools, raw materials and the skills to mek one. The wood came the woodwork department. The steel for the runners came from outside mi Dads workshop. It wer just rusty scrap layin ont floor.

The reason the metal fer the runners wer outside, is because mi Dad purram theer to go rusty. Then when they wer rusty. He would gera chitty off foreman, an claim it as scrap. So, when he took em home. He just handed the chitty in to security. Then he wunt be accused of nickin em.

The wood followed a similar path. Cut to size and shape and then muckied up a bit, and claimed as off cuts fer fire wood. All the accumulated bits wer then assembled into a sledge, when he arrived home. **A bit like Ikea does now.**

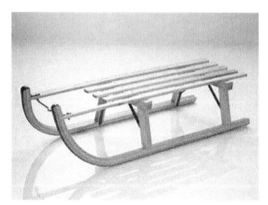

If you've never bin sledgin, you don't know what yer missin.

Today's Health and Safety brigade would be goin mad tryin to protect the dainty Snowflake society of today.

We used to sledge down the Side field it wer nice and steep and it wer long enough to get a good speed up.Usually on the first day of sledging, the track would be quite slow, but when the snow became compressed and frozen over night it became like a sheet of glass.Then you could really belt down the track at a great rate of knotts.

Shut yer eyes for this bit if yer from health and safety.

When the track wer ice we would have races to se who had the fastest sledge.The race would be a furious affair. No rules. All line up behind your sledge at top of the slope. Run like bloody hell, dive on yer sledge bellyflop, and pray. If yer dint crash, and yer managed to gerin front and stay theer.

You'd win. This in itself caused a problem. Ya see sledges don't have brakes, and where the track ended, there was nowt to stop yer runnin on to Canklow Road. **The main road from Rotherham.**

So. In order to win. You'd go to be the fastest thing on sheet ice. Wi no brakes, and likely end up under a Double Decker Bus

Na am going to go "Off Piste " a bit here. But to me its important. So bare with mi.

Was it a Lie or because of The Official Secrets Act

The way you dressed for sledging, was as important then, as it is today. Only we did not have the Hi Tec gear of t today. It was shall we say a little basic.

First. Two pair of socks, to keep yer hands warm. Dint work for long as soon they got wet they wer worse than useless.
Second. Two pair of socks to keep your feet warm. Dint work for same reason as them on yer hands. **Third.** Wellies. These wer allus a problem for us youngans. You see we wer still in short trousers, and the wellies rubbed on yer skin, just below the knee, and you'd probably not notice the pain this caused till you went to bed that night.

Fourth. Jumpers, as many layers as you could geron.
Fifth. Headwear. **And the reason for this diversion.**

Being only a few years after the end of WW2. Adults rarely talked about the war, and the parts they played in it. But boys being boys, used to brag about what their Dad did in the war. Most of mi mates, no, all of mi mates dads, served in the Army. Except mi Dad. He served in the Royal Air Force.

Now mi Dad never told mi wori did in the R.A.F. Buras far as I was concerned, there wer only one job int R.A.F. Yes. I telled mi mates he wer a Spitfire Pilot. Mi mates dint believed mi when a telled em. They sed a wer lyin an ad got to prove it.

Na there wer no way ad ever been able to prove it. That was until I wore my sledgin headgear

Mi Dad in his R.A.F. Uniform

One particularly cold winter. Mi Dad came outside as a wer off sledgin, an ses "here tha ar, sumat to keep thi head and ears warm. Then hands me a genuine Fighter Pilots Helmet, complete with microphone attachment and big padded lug hole protectors.

NOW WHAT MORE PROOF COULD YOU NEED.

Mi Dad really wer a Spitfire Pilot.

68

It wasn't till I recently applied for his service record from the Royal Air Force. I found out that throughout the war, my Dad was stationed at Millom Airbase Barrow-in-Furness, and worked as a Fitter and never wer able to fly a plane.

O.K. Maybe not a Spitfire Pilot . But still My Hero. And to all my mates. Sorry lads it weren't a lie. It wer top secret and we wer sworn to the Official Secrets Act.

1954 The Queens Visit. An It's A Good Job A Weshed Mi Neck

Alma Road School, where I wer at. Arranged for all the kids to line up on Sheffield Road, to wave flags, and cheer for Her Majesty the Queen, as she was driven past. On her way to Sheffield. Na a dint know much abart Queens and Kings, in fact the only other Queen a new owt abart wer that one called Baldy Seeya.

An a only remember her cos she had a daft name. Apparently, she's changed it, probably by deed poll, to Boudica. An a can see why.

Back to preparations for Her Majesties visit. Flags were made in class. To celebrate the occasion. Mothers Pride Bakery wrapped their sliced bread loaves in Union Jack, grease proof paper. Which we collected and made into flags and bunting.

Dress code wer strict.

Best trousers. No patches on arse end, no snake belts, just braces. Shoes Black no holes in soles. Shirt long sleeved White, no snot on cuffs. Hair weshed an tidy, plenty of Brycream, an a left side partin. No tide marks on yer neck. An wi gora special visit from Nitty Nora the Nit Nurse bura don't know why. Perhaps they thought we gi the Queen nits.

I wer hopin this visit wer goin to be worth all this fuss.

The Big Day arrives. All the kids gleaming n smart. A dint recognise most or em, ad never seen em this clean before. The whole school wer duly marched darn to Sheffield Road. A journey of no more than half a mile. We wer then lined up in rows by the roadside. I got pur on front row. A wer goin to ger a great view of our new Queen. A wer chuffed to bits. Ad av a reyt story to tell mi Dad, cos he ant even seen a Queen either.

While we waited for the motorcade to arrive, we practiced cheerin an waving ar flags. Na you know what kids are like. If sumat dunt happen instantly, they get bored. Well the Queen must av stopped for a cuppa tea, cos after five minutes of standin around on a cowd October mornin, she'd not arrived. Na ar wer waitin patiently, but Mick Rawson, who wer behind mi, wer gerin fed up, an started pokin mi int ribs, which dint bother mi first time he did it. Bur after he'd dun it 4 or 5 times ad ad enough. So a turned round n gin him a reyt gobfull.

At the very same second the Queen went past, apparently waving to all us kids. So because of Mick Rawson I never saw the Queen, and she only saw the back of mi ead. Bur at least mi neck wer clean and ad no patches on mi arse end of mi trousers. An the Queens never seen mi since.

70

Summers Endin An Am Off Up To "The Big School"—But Not Before I Stop Smokin

How to Stop Smokin When You Are 10 Years Old

You'll be glad to know that before a went up to big school ad managed to stop smokin. This in most part was thanks to Joe Guest.

Mind you it wer his fault a started smokin int first place.

A gang of us wer in the storage shed at the back of the Co-Op. We sorta used it as a gang hut when Co-Op wer shut.

One night, Joe gora packet of cigs out. Probably borrowed em of his older brother Ray. He sed "anybody want one". All tother lads grabbed one an lit up, an puffed away.

At this stage ad never ad a fag before, bura darn't chicken out. Now Joe knew ad never smoked, so gave me instructions. "Tek a deap drag" ses Joe "n when tha's gorra gobfull o smoke swallow it, an then blow it art". Well a did just as he sed, a great gobfull o smoke, swallow blow art.

Mi head starts spinnin, the rooms spinnin, the lads r shoutin "his gone green", "his gone green", "shift his gunna chuck".

They wer right I chucked, an chucked, an av never touched a fag since.

I often wondered what the Co-Op staff thought when they went into the store and found the decorations I'd left.

Am Still On The Way To The Big School, but not before I become a hero.

I Become A Hero "Sort Of"

I'm going to write this section very quietly cos not many people know about this.

The summer was ending and the trees were taking on their autumn hue.The bracken in Canklow Woods had gone from bright green to rusty brown. Now I think I ought to inform you,

in case you don't know. Bracken, when its brown, burn's very easily.

I may not have told you this before, but lads from Canklow seem to have a way with matches and are very adept at starting fires. There's nothing wrong starting fires, if it's in the right place. In fact it's essential if you happen to have a coal fire in your home. Which most people had.

Mi Mam allus telled mi never play wi matches. She never telled mi why a shunt play wi matches, so a ignored her. I wer amazed at her ability to allus know when ad bin lightin fires when ad bin art playin. Thinkin back it may av been the black sreaks runnin darn mi face from smoke gerrin in mi eyes, or it could av been that a stunk like a bonfire an she could smell mi two streets away, that gin it away.

Anyway back to mi heroism

We'd bin playin in Canklow Woods. Me, Chris Bell, john n Alan
Senior and Martin Melia. Yes "The Chain and Anchor Gang.

Well we started a fire int bracken. **Yes that brown bracken that burns
well**. Just a little fire, well tiny really, compared to some of fires we'd
ad.

We wer abart to purritart, when a bloody gret wind kem from no weer.
Well this little tiny fire, suddenly spread. Well, like wildfire. It wer
spreadin an gerin bigger by the minute. We took us cooats an jumpers
off, an tried to beat it art.

Burrit wer no good. It wer still spreadin an gerrin worse. It wer then
that Chris sed "wid berra get Fire Brigade."

We legged it darn to Dr Who police Box on Canklow Road, an phoned
Fire Brigade.They arrived pretty quick, an we shown em where this, by
now, bloody great big fire wer.

Bloody Big Fire

They gin us all shovel and asked us to help purit art. Which we willingly did. When it wer all art, they thanked us fer helpin, an said we shud become firemen when we gor owder, as we'd done such a good job.

A said it wer or reyt fer them bur I'm goin to gera good hidin wen I gerin, cos a stink a smoke. An mi mam will think av bin playin wi matches. Don't worry ses one er em. Ger int truck, we'll teck the home an explain to thi mam wora Hero thas bin.

An Hero. Me an Hero.

Me An Hero

Mi Mam wer chuffed to bits wi wor ad done, and med mi a cup of hot Ovaltine and a plate of biscuits before a went to bed. An that wer a dam sight better than gerin a thick good hidin.

Na a know what yer thinkin "you bloody stated it" well yes we did, burif we ant started it, we wunt of been able to become Heros purin it art, wud wi. An nobdy knows we started it except Me, Chris, Alan, John, n Martin and now you

After Summer Holidis when ya went back ta school the Teacher would allus mek us write a composition "think they call it an essay nowadays" entitled "What I did in the school Holidays" Funny a could only ever manage half a page.

Next mi most embarrassing memory.

How To Make A Kid From Canklow Glow Red.

A became friends wi a kid called Billy McMahon a think his Mam n Dad took pitty on me, cos they took me every weer wi em, even on holllidi. A suppose they would be classed as middle class in today's society. Mrs. McMahon wer a teacher, a dint know what Mr. McMahon did bur he had a posh car it wer an Austin A40 Somerset.

A learned a lot from the McMahons, they quietly introduced me into a world I knew nowt abart. The fact that they were Spiritualists may have something to do with it. They introduced me to a group of people, socially different to me, dint swear, dint shout an ball, always talked nice.

They had a Chapel on Percy Street just off Doncaster Gate. From here they ran a kind of Kids club, different to any weer else ad been. They had a choir. and put on plays that people paid to come and see. I still remember my stage debut. It wer Alice in Wonderlands "Mad Hatters Tea Party" I wer the Doormouse. I even remember mi stage directions. Dormouse takes head out of teapot and says "what time is it". Dormouse puts head back in tea pot.

It wernt a starring role bur everybody's got to start somewhere a suppose.

Oh! I also played the part of "A Portly Gentleman" in Charles Dickens A Christmas Carol.

It wernt till years later that a found out that a "Portly Gentleman" wer just another name for a fat bloke. Ee yer live an learn so they say.

Now to the embarasin bit.

Sometimes they would hold a general knowledge quiz, in which most of the kids took part in. Mrs McMahon said a should have a go.

Why not, am streetwise an think av gorra grasp of whats goin on.

You had to stand on stage, in front of all the mums and dads. Where a bloke would ask you questions. It wer like bein on 64000 Dollar Question wi Hughie Green.

When it got to my turn the bloke doin the Hughie Green bit ses to me. "John please can you complete the following famous saying"? **"Mind your Ps and .... ?**

A dint have to think long abart this one. The only thing I know that goes with peas is potatoes.

What a great Question.

"Potatoes" came my spirited reply.

The whole place erupted into hysterical laughter, an a ant gorra clue why. By the time the laughin finally stopped, ad gone bright red an a could feel mi face burnin like it wer n fire, a wanted to get the hell off the stage as fast as a could. The quizmaster looked at me, still laughin an ses "sorry wrong answer John". **The correct answer is "Qs".** **"Mind your Ps and Qs"**

What kind of answer is that? **What the bloody hell has Queues got to do wi Peas.**

A wer devastated.

Embarrassed, yes. Did a wished the ground would open up an swallow mi, yes. This one episode, more than any other in my life, made me realise how great the gap in social graces and education was between Canklow and the remainder of Rotherham.

You will be pleased to know I have nearly recovered from the trauma of this incident, acted out over 62 years ago, but still consider my answer was best.

Feyt or Run

A mentioned earlier there wer the occasional skirmish that resulted in a feyt.

In Canklow if tha wernt a good feyter tha ad better bi a good runner cos they wer thi only two choices.

Na av allready telled yer a wernt a good runner, well a wernt a good feyter either. An because a wore specs, a wer allus goin to be a target. "Who tha lookin at specy four eyes" wer the usual invitation to a feyt.

A wunt back darn from a feyt bura ad a distinct disadvantage. You see mi Dad said if tha gets in a scrap mek sure tha teks thi specs off. So thi don't get brock. Well that's all well an good, but wiart mi specs a wer almost blind, so it dint matter how good a cud feyt if tha can't see who tha feytin tha not goin to win.

Here's a couple of perfect examples of not being able to feyt mi way art a wet paper bag.

On a rare day that mi Dad had a day off, he decided to tek us for a Day art. when a sey us a mean mi Mam ar Kathryn an me, ar Pete wer courtin again. We went to Milhouse's Park in Sheffield. It wer a great place to gu, it ad a swimmin pool (nora paddlin pool like Clifton Park) and a kids playground.

That's weer the trouble started, this kid started pickin on mi little sister, ar Kate, well a wer avin non o that, so avin no more to do a picked a feyt wi im , an seein as he wer smaller than me, a reyt fancied mi chances. That wer till mi dad appeared. He charged up like a mad bull an shouts to mi "gis thi glasses" grabbed mi specs off mi face an buggers off. Leavin me to ger a reyt pastin, off the other kid, cos a wer as blind as a bat wi art mi specs.

A never went back to Millhouses ever agean.

Da ja vu Millhouses all over again

Livin in a terraced house in Canklow meant you wer able to use the passage between the houses to raise the volume of yer voice when yer ran through shoutin "Hi Ho Silver away" while slapin your pretend horse after watching Lone Ranger on TV. An when yer ger art onto street, all yer mates av dun same, an so it starts, the gun feyt at the OK Corral. Aimin yer two fingered pretend gun at yer nearest rival. Trev Haynes wer first n to tek aim at me, an shouts bang yer dead, so a do the Jimmy Cagney dyin bit an fall t floor.

Trev runs over to check to mek sure am dead, when I jump up an sey "ya missed mi" n shoot him." "A dint miss" ses Trev, "yer did" ses me, "a dint", "yer did", "a dint", "yer did", this went on for a bit then Trev gis mi a shuv, so I gis im a bigger shuv. Next thing it's fists at the ready, an the shout gus up from tothers ont street, FEYT, FEYT, FEYT.

A ring of kids suddenly surrounds us, that's when a realised we wer within earshot of r house, an mi dad ant gone to work yet.

Out runs mi dad "gis thi glasses, don't want thi breaking them", he teks mi glasses an disappears back inta house. Leavin me t feyt Trev.

It dint tek long, Trev smacked mi straight ont nooas. Caught mi on mi bind side (wi art mi glasses every side wer mi blind side) blood comes spurting art, feyt over. Trev lends mi his shirt sleeve to wipe blood off mi face and guides mi home to get mi glasses back.

NA THAT'S WHAT REAL FRIENDS ARE FOR.

Chapter 4 The Big School.

Yes av got Theer

South Grove Secondary Modern,

Entering Big School was ominous, especially for a kid still in short trousers. You wer a dead cert for the "First year clip" this wer an excuse for older kids to gi you a clout round ead, an it dint matter how you tried to avoid em theyd get yer. But by next year it would be my turn to dish it art, sumat to look forward to a suppose. It wernt as traumatic as Junior School, as first days go, but none the less a wer nervous.

We wer allocated our classes and introduced to our form teachers. Our teacher Mr. Price had a Welsh accent and a soft voice. A thought, he's a bit quiet for a teacher. A can't see him controlling us lot.

As I looked round the new class, it became clear ad been separated from most of me mates from Canklow. Colin Bonser and Ed Willey were the only two a recognised. The others wer all new faces to me. Worst of all some er em wer GIRLS. This was the first year South Grove had mixed classes. I don't know if I was pleased or disappointed time only would tell.

My estimation of Mr. Prices ability to control a class was totally unfounded. With his quiet Welsh voice and even temper, not only was he able to control the class. He was able to do his job and teach.

The debt I owe to this one man is immense, and for who, I hold nothing but praise.

Unfortunately, not all teachers were the same. As I was to find out during the following years.

Thats me bottom row second from left. Yes the one wi specs on.

The schooling I quite enjoyed, well most of it. Except for anything that included sport or logarithm's and History. I hated History. The class was taken by a teacher call Theodore Firth. He'd gora gob like Brian Blessed shoutin through a foghorn. Eyes int back er is head, and would score a direct hit between yer eyes, wi either chalk, or blackboard rubber. Whichever he happened to be using at the time. Oh! An he was also partial to laying the cane on your backside. Or on your bare legs if you happened to be wearing short trousers, as I often did.

Six Of The Best

I was punished quite a few times throughout my years at South Grove. Of all the times I had been punished, there was only one incident where I can recall the reason for the punishment. It was the ultimate punishment. Administered by the Head Master, "The Six of the Best", don't know why it had to be six, why not five or seven. No it was always six of the best, and come to think of it why was it the Best? The reason for this punishment, I thought was an overreaction, to an incident that happened in a woodwork lesson.

A lesson I happened to like.

We were learning how to do a mortise and tenon joint. You don't have to know what a mortise and tenon joint is, you just need to know that it takes **patience and skill to perfect. Attributes that wer not my strongest.**

The only tools you need to carry out this complex joint is a big wooden mallet and a mortise chisel.

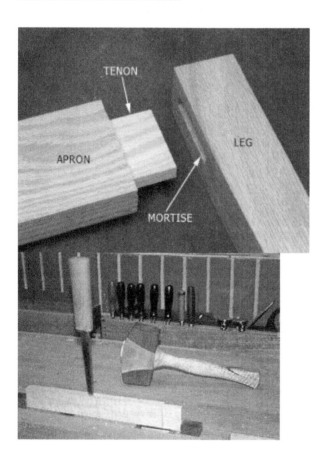

The scene is set

A piece of wood is clamped in the vice. An area was marked out as to where the wood is to be chiseled out. This performed, as shown by Mr. Hopkinson the Woodwork teacher. By gently tapping the chisel with the mallet, removing small slithers of wood each tap. This would eventually lead to a slot being cut into the wood.

That's where the problems started. The "gently tapping" and the "eventually" bit. My patience was at best, a bit on the short side.

I thought this tap, tap, tap, idea was much too slow. So, to speed things up a bit, I wedged the chisel in the wood, took the mallet in both hands. Like a Viking, took aim, and with one almighty blow crashed mallet down onto the chisel. Now I thought steel chisels were un-brekable, burra wer wrong. As soon as the mallet hit the chisel, the chisel snapped in two. Half the blade stuck deep in the piece of wood. The other half, including the handle went hurtling through space, endin up embedded in the wall next to the teachers desk The teacher went mad. Ordered mi to go to the Headmasters Study immediately, and wait there until he came up after class.

There were two lads waiting to see the Headmaster in front of me when a got theer. An they offered to let me go first. Burra told em I ad to wait for mi teacher to come, an a thanked them for the offer. When the two lads came out, they wer roorin like big babbies.

A thought to misen. A bet there from Broom Valley.

When Mr. Hopkinson arrived, he grabbed mi by mi lughole, an slung me in front of the headmaster, Mr Williams, another Welshman. The teacher demanded I be treated to "Six of the Best". The Headmaster asked for the reason for such a severe punishment. The teacher said ad "almost killed him wi a chisel". He said it wer "wanton thuggery", the chisel had missed his head by a fraction of an inch, and I deserved the maximum penalty.

To be fair to headmaster, he did ask me if I agreed with what the teacher had said.

No, a dint agree, a sed, he wer exaggerating. It wernt a fraction of an inch it missed him by, It wer nearer to two inches a sed. Dint do any good "Six of the Best " dished out. It hurt like hell, burra dint go out roorin like them lads from Broom Valley, cos a wer a kid from Canklow.

Oops! Av Ad An Accident

While still in the first year. I had a small emergency in the classroom. Having been out at playtime, playing marbles in the school yard. I came back to the classroom, with my winning marbles collection in my hand.

One of which was a large marble sized silver ball bearing.

As the lesson progressed, I got bored and I think I may have started to daydream. Anyway, for some reason, and I don't know why. I put the silver marble in my mouth. No, I still don't know why.

Mr Price must have noticed I wasn't paying attention, at which point he shouts "BROGAN" which startled me, and caused me to swallow the metal ball bearing. Panic sets in, but Mr. Price handles it well, gets the school nurse, who in turn gets the ambulance. Off to Hospital I go.

Me Mam arrives at the Hospital. Welcomes me with "whats tha bin upto now" I explained what had happened, an she wer just about to belt me round ead, when the Doctor came in, stopped her mid clout. Right said the Doctor we have done an x-ray, and the ball bearing does not seem to be lodged in a dangerous position. Natural movement will see it through in the next couple of days.

The Doctor took mi Mam to one side and whispered in her ear. I don't know what he said but I saw her pull a reyt funny face.

Well this explanation received a blank look from me and mi Mam. When we got home, mi Mam told me that I had to stay off school till the ball bearing came out. Then she progressed to tell me exactly where it was going to come out from. Yuk.

85

In order to ensure it had passed through. Every time I wanted a poo, I had to do it in an enamel potty. Left over from when our Kathryn was little.

Each time mi Mam had to examine the poo to see if the ball bearing had arrived. Well I will tell you this, she wasted her time doing the examining. Because when it came out, it wer like firein a musket ball. It took a gret lump of enamel off the potty, and you could have heard the clang two doors down.

Another lesson learned ball bearings belong in "bearings" not in yer gob

Mam Cana Have A Bike Part 1

The Bitsa

Fed up of walking to school I thought it was time I had a bike. All mi mates had bikes and of course our Peter had a bike.

86

A President Is Set

Our Peter had a Carlton Racer wi a Ten speed Deraila gears, drop handlbars and a racing seat that nearly cut you in two, and he wer a member of Rotherham Wheelers Cycling Club. So a president had been set.

Timin wer allus essential when you ask for summat that's goin to cost money, lots of money. The First Port of Call The first Port of Call would be mi Mam. Mam cana have a bike? "ask yer Dad am busy". Good result she dint say no.

First obstacle out of the way.

Next challenge Mi Dad. Now we all know mi Dads happiest on Sundis, we don't know why hes happiest on Sundis, he just is.

Plan of action. Gerim after Sundi dinner, but before his afternoon nap.

Dad cana av a bike? "al see na bugger off am avin a nap". Result! "al see" is as close as you get to a promise off mi Dad. Next day after school am off round all the bike shops of Rotherham. Collecting brochures to drool over. After hours of deliberation. The final three came down to a of three. First choice Carlton, 2nd Raleigh, and 3rd maybe a Claude Butler at a push.

Next day a telled mi Dad mi preference's in the same order. He sort of half listned cos he wer watchin 6 a clock news ont tele, so a left it wi him, an waited for mi bike. Na ad been a bit savvy, cos this wer about 12 weeks before Christmas. So I held back on any other Christmas requests to boost mi chances of gerrin a bike.

Christmas came, and as usual I woke up at the crack of dawn. A looked around mi bedroom to see if a could see owt that wer bike shaped. Nothin, I opened mi eyes wider, perhaps ad missed it. No, nowt. Perhaps they wernt able to gerrit upstairs. Yes, that ad to be the problem. A sneaked down stairs. Managing to stand on every stair that creaked. I opened the kitchen door as quiet as a could, but that creaked like one of them doors in an old castle. So much for being quiet.

I looked round the kitchen in the half light, and saw that in front of the fireplace stood a bike shape, covered in wrappin paper. A switched the big light on to get a better look. There was a label on it that said "Merry Christmas to our John from Mum and Dad". Well a wer in like Flynn, paper ripped off, to see mi bike in its full glory.

My astonishment wer underwellming. It wernt a Carlton like ar Pete's. It wernt a Raleigh either. Nor worrit a Claude Butler. No it wora Bitsa. It ad got bitsa this and bitsa that. Made from about five different bikes.

It had a grocers shop deivery bike frame. The front wheel were off a racing bike, that wer about 2 inches bigger than back wheel. So it looked like it wer goin uphill, even when it wer on the level. Don't know what the saddle wer off, it had great big springs that made you feel like you wer sat on a mattress. Unlike our Pete's 10 speed Deraila gears, this had a 4 speed Sturmey Archer gears. Of which only 1st and 4th worked, an if yer wernt careful when changin em, yer had no gears at all. Which caused the pedals just to spin, an if you happened to be standin on't pedals when this happened. It would cause a certain part of the male anatomy to come crashing on to the crossbar.

Brought many a tear to my eyes did that.

In all my excitement ad not noticed that mi Mam an Dad had crept up behind mi. "Happy Christmas" came the shout. "What do you think of it?" mi Mam asks. Yer Dad made you that Do you like it?"." Like it?" a said "its brilliant, how many other kids can say their Dad made em a bike for Christmas".

Now I know I didn't get my chosen bike.

But as mi Dad allus said 3rd class cyclin is better than 1st class walkin. Point taken.

That Place Wi Three Legs And Cats Wi No Tails

Nearing the end of my school days I got the opportunity to go on a School organised Holiday to the Isle of Man. This was my first trip abroad,

Go abroad to the **ISLE OF MAN**

Trains from all parts connect with steamers at Liverpool throughout the year and also at Fleetwood and Ardrossan during the summer. Please ask for details of services and fares.

I was travelling without parental restrictions, in charge of my own money, and along with a group of friends that I had grown close to over the previous years. I did not know what to expect of the Isle of Man, and I don't think the Isle of Man knew what to expect from a group of kids from Rotherham, where, the closest thing you could compare them to, was The Bash Street Kids from the Beano.

The journey was not dissimilar to the Club Trip, except for the inclusion of a four hour sea trip. The Canklow stomach held up well while the lads from Broom Valley and Herringthorpe where throwing up no sooner than we left Liverpool Docks.

Do a Believe in Fairies?

From the Ferry it was a short coach ride to the resort of Port Erin. With one stop en-route, at a place called Fairy Bridge.

Na apparently a Fairies live under the bridge. Well a dint see a fairy, and nor did anybody else. When a gor home, a telled mi Dad about these here fairies. An he sed ad "more chance of seein a fart in a blanket". Well a must say, av never seen one o them either. .

The Old Fairy Bridge
The Isle of Man

What Bloody Fairies???

Staff what Staff?

Our accommodation for the Holliday was to be a school in between Port Erin and Port St Mary.

The classes had been made into dormitories filled with camp beds for our stay. We were to be supervised throughout our stay by Staff from South Grove School, who traveled with us. The supervision they provided, was to say, in the least, "limited", in fact it was so limited, the only time I can ever recall seeing any staff member on a regular basis was at feeding time.

That meant a lot of unsupervised spare time for certain mischievous little monkeys to do their worst. My aim is not to embarrass or incriminate any of the people who were with me on that holiday, so Arthur Clover, Edmund Willey, Jimmy Everett and may be Frank Oxspring I will keep your names out of it for a small fee.

The Deep Blue Sea.

The thing I remember most was the clarity of the sea. You could see your feet even when the water wer up to your neck. Unlike Cleethorpes where you couldn't see your toes when the water was up to your ankles.

All my life as far back as I can remember I have loved going fishing, so coming to a place where fishing was a way of life was like heaven to me. Most of the holiday I was in, on, or under the sea.

As I was brought up on river fishing I was going to have to learn a new skill set to be able to catch sea fish.The first new skill was using a hand line, which as the title suggests is using a line and your hands to catch fish. After purchasing said handline and bait from the local tackle shop in Port Erin, it was a short walk along the Pier to the lighthouse that protected the bay.

Typical Handline

Some of the lads had done this type of fishing before, so they gave me instructions on what to do. The handline is a H frame, about the size of a large hand with a big ball of string wrapped round it. At the end of the string are attached the hooks and a large lead weight. Right the skill bit.

You bait the hooks with your chosen bait, remove all the string off the handle. The more string you've got, the further out you can throw your bait. The lead weight on the end of your line has 2 purposes. First the weight of the lead gives the ability to get a good distance away from the Pier. Secondly it provides resistance when a fish bites letting you know its grabbed your bait.

Now for the fun bit.

To get your bait out into the sea you have to throw it, but not any old way. You take your hooks and weight and about 2 foot of line and let it dangle from your hand. Face the sea, start to spin the string in your hand, like a windmill, when its spinning like hell, let it go launching it at the sea.

All of which I did perfectly so perfect that everybody was amazed at the speed and distance that was being traveled. That's when somebody shouts thi handles gone wi thi line. Yes there it was following the string hurtling towards the sea.

Yes I had learned how to use a hand line, and I also found out you need to hang on to the other end of the string. Ah well you live and learn.

We can Do the Conger.

The Fishing theme continued throughout the holiday, and quite successfully. We went out on the fishing boats where the tackle was provided and instructions provided by proper fishermen. The result being that we caught Mackerel and Pollack in abundance. So much so we were able to provide fish for meals at the school and receive a small income from the local fishmonger. After my handline cock-up I was left with 2 choices as to be able to carry on fishing. 1 Spend another 2/6 on new handline or 2 Find the one I had lost. What does a typical Yorshireman do? We all know the answer, off wi mi keks belt along Pier straight off the end and into space. It wer just like going off top block at new baths. Bura med sure nobody wer swimmin under water this time,

See a followed mi own advise, a looked before leapin.

Now I must not be the first person to have lost his handline cos whoever invented them made them out of wood so they would float, and sure enough 100 yards from the pier was my bright yellow handle floating on the sea. Phew 2/6 saved.

The title above "We Can Do The Conger" relates to the scariest day of the Holiday.

Near the main Pier at Port Erin was a small jetty that protruded about 30 yards into the sea, and in such a place that even at low tide there was a depth of water deep enough to fish in. Like everywhere else the water was gin clear except, that because the water never receded, there was masses of seaweed so you could not actually see the bottom. One of the boat skippers that we had been out with told us that this area is a likely place to catch a Conger eel. I had only ever seen pictures of a Conger Eel and they looked ugly and ferocious but wer up for a challenge as usual.

We wer told we needed a big hook and the best bait would be a fish head. So suitably prepared, a fish head from the local fishmonger and a promise of a bob a foot if we caught one, a hook that looked like it belonged on Captain Hooks hand.

Four of us set off doing the conga.

Like most kids fishing is only fun when you are catching fish. When you are not catching fish its boring and that's when you start messing about. Well we had reached the messing about part, by seeing who could chuck the fish head and hook farthest. My first go wer rubbish, it only went a few feet from the edge and began to sink to the bottom.

From out of nowhere there was such a commotion, a Conger Eel came out of the seaweed in front of our eyes, grabbed the fish head, and was off like a shot. The line was disappearing like it wer being pulled by a train. We all grabbed for the line that's when we realised we had bit off more than we could chew. As the line tightened the true strength of the fish became apparent. Four of us were hanging on to a fish with the pulling power of a steam train and a set of teeth that could eat one of us whole.

A Reyt Gob Full Of Teeth

We need a plan.

First idea cut the line. No good. The knife was on the roadside 20 yards away and it needed all four of us to stop the fish pulling us in. Second idea try to shake the hook out. No good. The hook was so big once it was in it was staying in. Third idea drag it up onto the jetty and up to the road where we could dispatch it using the knife.

Now that stands a chance.

Idea three adopted we managed to drag this creature onto the jetty. That's when we see what a fearful thing we had caught. It was as thick as a drainpipe about four foot long a mouth chocka block wi teeth. It was thrashing abart like a flag in a gale. We now needed to get this thing up to the road. It was going to take all four of us to pull it up the jetty, but somehow I had got separated from the other three in the mayhem.

The situation was, the other three lads were facing the roadside, hanging on to the line trying to drag the fish. I was between the thrashing Conger Eel and the end of the jetty. It was at this point that one of the lads reminded me of a fisherman's tale that mi Dad told us.

He told us that if you catch an eel you can stop it from wriggling by stunning it. All you need to do is strike it hard at the end of its tail. Now that's O.K. when it's a six inch long and thin as a boot lace, but when its four foot of muscle and your between it and the deep blue sea, it's not a good time to test one of mi Dads theories. So I dismissed that idea with a few well-chosen Canklow words.

Luckily a bloke had been watching our exploits and decided to lend a hand. With his help and having reached safety, the fish was humanly dispatched. At this stage we decided to hold the fishmonger to his promise. The four of us slung the eel over our shoulders and marched off singin "we can do the conga da da da der", into a very surprised fishmongers. Who true to his word gave us a bob a foot. We returned to our dorms covered in fish slime but four bob richer.

Jeremy Wade would have been proud.

Chapter 5. A Transformation Begins

The Working Man Becomes A MOD.

I had reached the age, in my case 15 years one month, to leave school behind, and venture off into the world of adulthood and work. Hold on a bit I've just found out somebody has just invented a whole new class of people, they come after school age, but before adulthood, and apparently called Teenagers.

I will deal with the work part first, because that more or less dictated what type of Teenager you became.

Before leaving school, like all the other kids, I was interviewed by the Career's Master. My interview was not going to take long. Past experience was guiding me in one of three directions. Top of the list was Fireman "Why Fireman" asks the Career's Master. "Well mainly because I am experienced at putting out fires". I replied. "Ah well" says the Career's Master " To become a Fireman you have to be 18 years old and you are only 15″ "and a month" I reminded him.

"Have you got a second choice" he asks "yes" I replied, "and what would that be" he asks. "A Lumberjack" was my confident reply. "Tell me er what's your name" "John" I replied. "Tell me John why do you want to be a Lumberjack". "Well I love chopping trees down" it seemed a reasonable answer, but he was giving me a puzzled look.

"How tall are you John?" "about five foot four" "and what do you weigh?" "nearly nine stone" "Ah well to become a Lumberjack, you need to be at least six foot tall and have a muscular physique. So I'm afraid that rules that job out. Do you have any other choices". "Yes I have one more choice" "what would that be"? " A Vicar" His face was a picture, it was obvious from his response that wasn't the answer he was expecting.

I know these may seem a diverse set of career choices, but to me it was a logical progression.

He put his thumb and forefinger across the bridge of his nose and sort of pinched himself and then shook his head. "Tell me" he said "I can't wait to hear this" he says "why a Vicar"? "Well when I was in confirmation class at the Vicarage the other week, I heard two of the clergy talking, and one said the Vicar earned £40 a week, and I thought my Dad who works at Steelos 7 days a week, earns less than half that. A vicar works one day and earns twice as much as mi Dad, which job would you rather have".

He was almost in tears and he had real trouble keeping his composure. I think he was sad because he had some bad news to tell mi. He started spluttering and I could see he was having difficulty getting his words out. When he finally spoke he said "Well John I have got some really bad news for you. You see to become a vicar you have to spend many years at University and unfortunately you do not have the qualification's to apply".

"How about I try to get you a job at Steelos, same place as your Dad". "That would be great" I said, and that's exactly what he did. I Started work at Steel Peach and Tozer on the Tues 26th Dec 1961 Aged 15 and nearly 2 months.

Mam Cana Hava Bike Part 2

Now I know what you're thinking " he's already got a bike" well just hold on, and don't get your knickers in a twist. All will become clear.

Having now started working and earning money it was time for a rebirth as a Teenager.

Canklow in the fifties had a major gang culture. Most of which was made up of Teddy Boys or Rockers. Teddy Boys dressed in their Crape Beetle Crusher shoes and Drape jackets with velvet collars and Rockers dressed in studded leather Flying Jackets, scruffy jeans and motor bike boots. Both groups had similar slick backed hairstyles which kept Brycream in business for years.

Well its now 1963. A band called The Beatles had released a record called "Love Me Do" at the back end of 1962 and in early 1963 another new band released a record called "Come On". This new band were called The Rolling Stones. You may or may not have heard of these bands, but they were on the crest of a wave. That was going to change the youth scene for ever, and that certainly included this Canklow Kid.

The transformation begins.

The Hairstyle First.

Down to Eric Duckers barbers shop at the bottom of Castle Avenue. Eric was a well-established barber that ran his business from his front room, but unlike more traditional barbers, Eric's barbers chair was in the centre of the room, also unlike most traditional barbers Eric's room had no mirrors.

What Eric did have though was pictures on the walls, of all the latest fashionable styles.

Eric was like a cross between Mr Teezy Weezy and Vidal Sassoon.

You walk into Eric's shop, Eric says "what you havin" "A Beatle Cut pleas Eric". "Fine sit int chair" Scissors and trimmer out and Eric's arms going like bees wings. He has no sooner started than he's finished **"anything for the weekend"** he says "no thanks" I reply, thinking one day I will ask him what I might need for the weekend?

"that'll be 1/6 thank you" I pays me 1/6 and walk up the street to our house, showin off my new Beatle cut to the World. Which I have not yet seen, due to the lack of mirrors in Eric's shop .

Our house has 2 main rooms downstairs, a kitchen, come dining room, come living room. The other room is for show, only to be used when mi Dad has a party on Boxing Day and when our Pete is courting.

The fireplace in the kitchen/dining/living room was a range type over which was a large mirror. So I arrive in the kitchen, wrestle mi way through the clothes hanging to dry from the ceiling rack, and take a look at Eric's work. **What the Fxxk is that. There it wer, a short back and sides wi a side parting.** You see it's the only style Eric could do. Time to change my barber sorry Eric.

Next In The Style Change,

The Clothes.

Down to John Collier "The Window To Watch" As the TV advert used to say.

Rotherhams Window To Watch "John Collier".

Jacket- Grey Fleck, Single Breasted, Single Vent, No Tab Pocket, 6 Buttons in 3 Pairs, Slim Collar.

Shirt- Candy Striped Ben Sherman slim fit, button down collar.

Threads- Falmer Straight Leg **NO turn up**

Next Down to Sylos for the Shoes.

Shoes -Crocodile skin winkle pickers, the more pointed the better, over white socks.

And of course the obligatory "American Parka wi fur round the hood" from Fieldsends Ex-Army Stores ont High Street.

Yes I'd become a MOD. Not just any MOD, but the only MOD in Canklow.

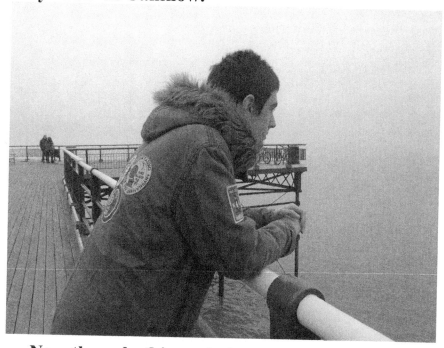

Now the only thing missing was "The Wheels"

Hence Cana Have a Bike 2

After my previous attempt at getting my dad to buy me a bike. "The Bitsa" I decided a different tack was needed. By now my dad was in his fifties, so the Sundi morning thing had died out. I needed a different plan to catch him when he was in a good mood. I thought Satdi tea time would be best, and fate would prove me right.

Satdi tea time arrived and I put the plan into action. "Mam cana hava bike" "ask yer Dad am busy". Right answer, I thought. Now to tackle my Dad. "Dad cana hava bike" "thas got one already" he says. "No not a push bike a want a motor bike" I replied. I had timed my questions to coincide with the football results coming onto the wireless, knowing full well that my Dad would only be half listening, while concentrating on his Littlewoods Pools.

He looked up from checking his football coupon, and with a smile, well more of a grin, on his face says, "maybe if a wint pools".

That wernt the answer a wanted, my Dad had done the pools for years and never won more than a few Bob. That was until that Satdi night. When he got 7 Draws and won £900. Yes am gerrin a Bike. One thing about my Dad, he lead by example, a promise was a promise.

If you remember last time I dint get any of my choices for my pushbike. Perhaps I caused confusion by having too many choices. Better make it easier by giving him just 2. I did not want to appear too choosy, so I said I would be happy with a second hand Lambretta or even a Vespa.

The thing I DID NOT want was anything resembling a Triumph or a BSA covered in grease and oil, and sounded like thunder on steroids.

After a few weeks of sleepless nights, the day came when my dad walked into the house and says "your brand new, not second hand, bike is on the yard". Brand new! Now I wernt expectin that. Out I go and there it is. Brand new still in plastic sheeting.

I ripped the sheeting off to admire my Brand New bike, I took a step back and gasped. I wernt expectin that. I know what you are thinking, you bet I got a Triumph or a BSA or some other Rockers machine, knowing I was a MOD.

But you would be wrong, although it wasn't a Lambretta or Vespa either.

There before my eyes was a brand spanking new 49cc Raleigh Runabout, with an engine capacity of an egg cup, that could reach a top speed of 25 mile per hour if you rode it off Flamborough Head in a following gale. The wheels were the same as a pushbike and it even had pedals to help you get up the slightest incline.

Yes! It Wer This

Disappointed, you are joking, I was mortified. What self-respecting MOD would be seen riding a 49cc, glorified pushbike through the Rockers "Hood" of Canklow. Mind you I would be safe from being attacked. They wouldn't be able to feyt for laughing at me. My mate Tony Hather still takes the pee, even today, 50 odd years later, about me, pedalling like hell, and him passing me, riding on his push bike going up Royds Moor.

need not have worried, a few months later, dignity was regained. The Raleigh Runabout was traded in for a second hand LAMBRETTA Series1 Li150, Yes result! I was finally a proper MOD.

A Reason to Leave

Along with the style change comes the hormonal change, and I start to notice those things called "GIRLS". Since starting work I had gained a new circle of friends, some of who come from areas I had never heard of like "Thurcroft" and "Dinnington". My new found freedom meant that I could visit these far flung places.

When I say far flung I mean no more than 15 miles.

I began to visit Dinnington quite often, mainly because they had a dance venue called The Lyric, which for some reason, was able to attract the top Bands and Groups of the day. The likes of Cilla Black, The Ivy League, Herman's Hermits, and many of the upcoming Liverpool bands. It was there, one Saturday night, that little bugger, Cupid stuck his oar in, and little did I know that my life was about to change for ever.

Dancing round her handbag, with a group of about 10 girls, was this beautiful blonde girl with big ......eyes. I noticed her eyes because they were above another big part of her anatomy, that boys of a certain age tend to notice. I managed to catch her eye while she was dancing, no she'd not dropped it, I gave her a smile which she shyly returned. Not being known for my shyness, I decided to go and have a chat and introduce myself. I walked over the dance floor towards her, and as I got closer she started to blush.

This was somewhat disconcerting, where I come from girls don't blush, and you knew where you stood with them, if they dint like you they would simply tell you to F off, so this was a totally new experience for me.

She was even more beautiful the closer I got, I was in love. After a short introduction, and not to interfere with her dancing, I asked her name and if I could walk her home after the dance. This had an immediate effect. The girls dancing round the handbags suddenly stopped dancing, even though the music was still playing. They made a tight circle round the handbags and summoned my new love to join them.

It wer like an all-female rugby scrum.

Every few seconds a head would pop up and look my way, and then pop down again. I had never seen this happen before, but then again I had never asked to walk a girl from Dinnington home before, so a thought it was a local custom.

I later found out that 8 of the girls dancing were my new loves sisters and cousins, and the dance floor meeting was to decide whether I was a worthy escort I must have passed because Sandra, that was my new loves name, agreed to let me walk her home.This was to be the beginning of the end of my life in Canklow.

Leaving the land of my father.

After my success at the Lyric, my love life was on the up. My now regular girlfriend, Sandra, was taking up a large amount of my attention, so much so that I had almost moved in. Sandra's parents treat me like the son they never had, and gave me more affection than my real parents.

A subject that never seemed come up in conversation in Canklow was Sex. To be more precise Sex Education. It would appear that parents expected teachers to explain "the birds and bees" thing, and teachers saw this as the parents responsibility, the result being the only sex education you got came from stories and exploits from the older boys.

I know your guessing where this is going but stay with me.

Twelve months on, the relationship was as strong as ever, but a blip was on the horizon. I had been selected, along with my then, best mate Maurice Hayden, to represent Steelos on a month's residential Duke of Edinburgh's Award course, at the Moray Sea School in the North of Scotland.

Up to this time we had not been separated for even a weekend ne mind a month. This could be the make or break of the relationship. We need not have worried the saying "absence makes the heart grow fonder" was proved to be right.

We wrote love letters, not Skype, Face Time, email, or messenger, almost every day we were apart.

Now when I got home, an remember, I had just spent the previous month in the Cairngorm Mountains, Sailed in force 10 Gales in the Pentland Firth, canoed the 22 mile Length of Loch Ness and cycled from coast to coast across Scotland. In all that time, in such a remote area, I hardly saw another human being, ne mind a female. To say I was excited at getting home and being reinstated with the love of my life would be a massive understatement.

It was about three months after my return from Scotland that Sandra announced she was pregnant. "How did that happen" I said.

Oh! Come on av already told you a dint av any sex education in Canklow. An I know what you are thinking,
A should have asked Eric Ducker for something for the weekend.

When the dust settled, we had the telling the parents problem. Sandra's parents were brilliant especially as we had decided to Wed. The same can't be said for my parents, all of a sudden my mother had taken on the status of "Lady of Canklow Manor." "I had brought utter disgrace on the family" she said.

This is a family that originated from the Peat Bogs of Ireland, and previously resided in the notorious Gorbals slums of Glasgow, and now lived on Castle Avenue in Canklow.

Once the disgrace bit subdued the Wedding date was set, the 27th of March 1965.

As March was the end of the Tax year, anyone who married in March, received a refund of Tax paid for a full year, see thrifty as ever.

Before the Wedding took place, Sandra has since told me. Her Mother gave her the option to call the wedding off without any repercussions. Which she declined.

My Mother on the other hand said "shes only a miner's daughter tha can do better than that", "well thas med thi bed tha mun lay in it" and finally "al gi thi six months before tha comes home.

Now here's the rub. My Mothers Father was a miner, I suppose that made my Mother "only a miner's daughter", just what I was Marrying, and as to the disgrace I had brought on the family, My Mother and Father Married in April 1934 and my Brother Pete was born in July 1934, you do the sums. And the six months she gave me, well in the words of the celebrated Rotherham comedian **Sandy Powell** "can yer hear mi Mother"

"Can yer hear mi Mother"

"am still laying in the bed a med, 54 years later".

I Left Canklow on my Wedding Day never to return except for the occasional visit. Did I miss the noise, smoke and the people, yes I did. The main difference I found between Canklow and Dinnington was the noise silence makes. Gone was the comforting and rhythmic dull thud from the heavy steam hammers of the drop forge, the whistles of the trains, and the clatter of the wagons of the shunting trains, replaced by................................**Silence**...........................so **loud**.

A new life begin post Canklow

Ad like to finish mi first book on a high and end on a positive note.

On How lucky av been in life. Especially how lucky av been when accidents appened.

119

In this book you've learned about mi fallin int river Rother an nearly drowdin int mud. About gerrin attacked by geese on holidi. An bein stranded and almost etten by a conger eel int Isle of Man.

Oh! A know a dint tell yer about the rope swing. and the Double Decker bus. But maybe a will in a later book.

The best an luckiest accident I had. I know lucky and accident are a bit of a misnomer, but bear with me, all will become clear, more or less.

This is how it appened.

I was now married and living in Dinnington, and wer ont nightshift at Steelos.. Before going on shift I would often call in to see my Mum and Dad, as it was on my way to work.

Owd on a minute. A must tell you this before a forget.

Me and Sandra had been married for about six month, when we went to Mums for tea. Yes the wipe on wipe off salmon sandwiches.

During a conversation with Sandra, mi Mam asked how Sandra was coping with married life.To which she responded "absolutely great, except for getting up to cook John's breakfast, like you used to do at 4.30 in a morning, before he goes on the dayshift". This comment received a shocked look off mi Mam. "You cook his breakfast like I used to do. I've never cooked him a breakfast in his life. And he dunt like meat anyway".

Here endeth my Early Breakfasts.

Back to my visit.

After one such visit. I left mi Mam an Dads house to make the short journey to work. Now if you have been paying attention. You will know I'm a Mod and as a Mod I ride a scooter "Mam cana av a bike 2".

Since getting married I had upgraded my scooter to the Mods dream machine a Lambretta GT 200. But because of lack of funds it was basic with none of the Mod bling. No mirrors, no spot lights, no chrome back rest, No fancy paint job.

That was until that lucky night. After leaving the house I traveled along Canklow Road It was about 9.30 at night and dark, but Canklow road was well lit. In front of me, going slow, was a flatbed lorry. As the road was straight and well lit I decided to overtake the lorry. I got almost halfway past, when I noticed a bright orange lamp on his front mudguard was flashing on and off continuously. Shit he's turning right. Then Bang, me and the scooter went under the side of the lorry and out the back. I remember my head banging along the causeway edge, but the rest was a bit of a blur. The lorry was no where to be seen.

The front wheel was pointing left and the handlebars facing right. Somehow I managed to return to my Mum and Dads house, walked through the door an sed av ad an accident, and promptly passed out.

I remember picking my scooter up, and manged to get it to start.

I had no injuries except for a couple of scrapes. My scooter though was a different story, it was wrecked. Fortunately my insurance company agreed to have it repaired, and delivered my pride an joy to the local scooter repair shop. I went along to the shop, to oversee the repairs. The workshop guy was also a Mod. He asked me if a would give him a free hand, when it came to the respray, giving me a nudge nudge, wink

wink. Like the chap on Monty Pyhon Show. Or did I want it back in its boring White with a Red stripe.

A Free hand? Absolutely no question.

I left the garage not knowing what I was going to receive on my return.

After about five weeks of waiting. I got a letter to say my scooter was ready for collection. I returned to the garage to pick up mi scooter. When I saw it I was stunned, not in the way that my other experiences had stunned me. You know the Bitsa and the Raleigh Runabout. No,standing in front of mi, was the most beautiful Mod machine I had ever seen. The body and legshields painted in dark metallic Porsche Purple with White unique graphics on the side panels, and front mudguard.

Finished of with enough chrome to sink a battleship. This was the ultimate Mod machine, a real crowd puller. The likes of which I had never seen before, or for that matter since.

The Replica I Built From My Box Of Bits Thanks to my wife
Sandra

Now you tell me that wernt a lucky accident. A dint die, and I
realised the ultimate Mod dream.
and as Kylie Sang. "I should be so Lucky, Lucky Lucky Lucky"

By the way not that Kylie that wer involved in mi sex scandal

"Keep The Faith and Ride Safe"

Glossary

Nah then, 'ere's a guide to chattin' reyt Yorkshire!

(Hello, here is a guide to proper Yorkshire dialect).

First tha's got to drop yer 'H' as in 'has' and 'her', and yer 'T' and tha dunt need a G in owt endin ING like swimin or fishin.

Here is a glossary of common Yorkshire Words n Phrases along with their meanings… Yorksher is not slang it's an accent, and a dialect.

A

Allus – meaning always. "I allus wesh mi ands before mi snap."

Am – meaning I am. "Am off t' Pub."

Arse/arse end/arsin abart, meaning The back of something or somebody making an idiot of themselves

B

Bagsy – meaning to claim something for yourself. "Bagsy me that Red one".

Bairn – meaning child. "The poor bairn needs a nap."

Belt – meaning hit. "Shut up or I'll belt yer!"

Be reyt – meaning it'll be okay. "it al bi all reyt."

Black bright – meaning very dirty. "He was black bright when he gor hom from t Pit."

Bog – meaning toilet. "I'm off t' bog."

Brew – a cup of tea. Preferably Yorkshire tea. "Ee am ready for a brew av gora gob like Gandis flip flop"

Bura– meaning but I "bura don't want to"

Butty – meaning sandwich. "Av got banana butties for mi snap".

C

Cack-handed – meaning left handed. "No wonder shi can't use cork screw reyt, shi's cack-handed."

Champion – meaning excellent. "Ee them theer buns wer champion!"

Chip oyle – meaning fish and chip shop. "Does tha want owt from t chip oyle?"

Chuffed – meaning happy, pleased. "I were well chuffed wi' me new boits

Coyal oyle or coal 'ole – meaning coal cellar. "Al put thi int coyal oyle if tha dunt behave thisen." Thanks to *Sharon Love* for this one

D

Dollop – a lump of something, usually food. "Can I have a dollop of mash wi me pie please?"

Down't (road) – meaning down the road. "Im off down't road, will be back in an hour."

E

Ead – meaning head. "Tha nowt burra big ead"

Eck – meaning hell. "Ooh blooming 'eck, that hurt?"

Eeh by gum – meaning 'oh my god'.

Eh – meaning what, or pardon, or an expression of confusion.

Ey up – meaning 'watch out', 'be careful', or to be used as a greeting, especially when seeing someone/something you weren't expected. "Ey up Lad! Not seen you in ages."

F

Faffin' – meaning messing about. "Stop faffin' wi thi dinner, n gerit etten, "

Fettle – meaning to make, tidy or mend. "that kitchens ready for a good fettling"

Feyt – An altercation or Fight "what tha starin at does tha want a feyt"

Flaggin' – meaning getting tired. "We ought to stop for a cuppa, I'm flaggin."

Flippin' eck – meaning bloody hell, a term of shock or surprise. flippin'eck! Where'd tha come from?"

Flit – to move house frequently. From old Norse. "We're flitting again this summer."

Flummoxed – meaning confused. "Well I'm flummoxed as to where me car keys went, I 'ad 'em in me 'and a second ago."

Friggin' – a curse, alternative to flaming, bloody, etc. "Friggin' ell, not again!"

G

Gander – meaning look. "Gis a gander at that!"

Ginnel/Genal/Passage – meaning alleyway. "They ran off down the ginnel!"

Gip – meaning retch. "That reeks, it's making me gip!"

Giz – meaning give me. "Giz it now!"

Goosegogs – meaning gooseberries. "Got a load of gogs to mek jam wi' this year."

Guff – meaning fart. "Who's guffed? It stinks!"

H

Hell Fire – meaning oh my god. "Hell Fire! When did this happen?"

I

In't – meaning in the. "They're in't bedroom weer ya left em"

In a bit – meaning goodbye, see you later. "I'm off t'pub al sithi in a bit"

J

Jammy – meaning lucky. "Tha won how much ont horses? Ya jammy sod"

Jiggered – meaning tired, exhausted. "No way am doin that, I'm jiggered."

K

Kegs/Kecks – meaning pants or trousers. "Where're me kegs? I need em for work."

Kiddin' – meaning joking. "Tha spent how much? Tha must be kiddin"

L

Lass – meaning girl, wife or woman. "Our lass is not comin out tonight"

Lug – meaning to pull or tug. "I had to lug me suitcase all the way home from t' station."

Lug 'ole – meaning ear. "gis yer lug'oles,I want to tell thi summat."

M

Manky – meaning disgusting. "That sandwich wer manky, must have been in there a month!"

Mardy – meaning moody. "Stop being such a mardy arse and come out!"

Maungy – meaning whiny, sulky. "He's always maungy when he's hungry."
Mek– meaning make " mi dad sed mek a cuppa"

Mind – meaning be careful. "Mind the traffic when tha crosses t'road"

Mingin' – meaning disgusting. "Have you seen the state of his room? It's mingin'."

Mitherin – meaning annoying or bothering. "Gerout from under mi feet n stop mitherin mi"

Monk on – meaning to be grumpy. "He got dumped last week so he's got a monk on."

Mi'sen – meaning myself. "I don't like cricket much mi'sen."

N

Narky – meaning moody, sullen, sulky. "She's narked off at sommat."

Nay – meaning no. "Nay lad, it's too late to go fishin'."

Nah then – meaning hello, dialect version of "Now Then". "Nah then! What tha bin up t'?"

Neb – meaning nosey. "Keep your neb out of my business!"

Nesh – meaning to feel the cold. "Nesh southerners, can't hack a Yorkshire winter!"   Nora– meaning- not a "thas nora chance of winnin"

Nowt – meaning nothing. "I've got nowt to do today. I'm bored."

Now then – meaning hello. "Now then! How about a catch up over a pint?"

O

Oh aye? – meaning oh really, or oh yes? "We're getting married next year". "Oh aye? Well congratulations!"

'Ow do – meaning how do you do? "'ow do love? You well?"

Owt – meaning anything. Opposite of nowt. "Have you bought owt for tea?"

P

Pack it in – meaning stop it. "Pack it in fighting you two or there'll be no pocket money for a month."

Parky – meaning cold. "It was a bit parky earlier so I put the fire on."

Playin' pop – meaning to get angry with someone or tell them off. "When I got 'ome our Keith were playin' pop wi' the neighbours for playin' their music so loud."

Pop – meaning fizzy drink "Get us a pop from t' shop."

Podgy – meaning a fat or chubby person. "She was podgy as a baby, but she's a beauty now!"

Put wood in t 'ole – meaning shut the door. "Put wood in t' ole, tha lettin' t'cold in."

R

Rank – meaning disgusting. "Urgh, Lancashire 'ot pot? that's rank."

Reckon – meaning to think or figure out. "What you reckon to the news, eh?"

Reeks – meaning it smells bad. "Hmm it reeks of eggs in 'ere."

Reyt – meaning right or very. "We had a reyt good night."

S

Sarnie –See Butty

Silin' – meaning raining heavily. "Am bloody wet through, it's silin' it down out there!"

Sithee – meaning Goodbye, see you later, contraction of See Thee. "Aye lad, Sithee!"

Snicket – Same as Ginnel

Sprog – meaning child. "She's having another sprog!"

Spuds – meaning potatoes. "Were having jacket spuds and beans for tea."

Spuggy – meaning sparrow. "I was the spuggy again on the bird table this morning."

Summat – meaning something. "I need summat to do at the weekend."

Sup – meaning to drink. "Sup up, we're off to the next pub!"

T

Ta – meaning thank you. "Ta very much. Keep the change."

Tarra – meaning goodbye. "Tarra love, see you next Sunday."

Tek – meaning take. "You're tekking the mick now."

Telled – meaning told "a telled yer it wer im"

Tha – meaning you. "Where's tha been lad? We've been worried about thi"

Thissen – meaning yourself. "How'd ya feel about it thissen?"

T'werk – where Yorkshire people go from 9-5 Monday to Friday. "I'm off t'werk love."

Tyke – meaning Yorkshire person.

U

Un – meaning one. "He's a reyt un, that bloke int Jag."

W

Wang – meaning to throw. "Wang it over here!"

Watter – meaning water. There is only one r in watter and that's at the end

While – meaning until. "I'm working while six tonight."

Wunt– meaning would not   "she wunt come in"

Y

Yonder – meaning over there. "What's that yonder I see?"

Printed by Amazon Italia Logistica S.r.l.
Torrazza Piemonte (TO), Italy

10604295R00079